B. G. Bhagee

Memories of a Colonial Childhood

Philippa Perry

PHILIPPA PERRY

ISBN-13: 978-1461192190

ISBN-10: 1461192196

LCC

DEDICATION

To: All of us who still remember

Author's Note

This is not a history text, just stories I have told many times. These are memories of my early life; all the events happened, they are true, to the extent that my memory can be trusted.

Some names were changed to protect me from the wrath of my relatives. Any resemblance to people living or dead is a mere oversight.

I am grateful to my long-suffering husband, Melvin, who persisted in collecting my tales and ruminations and designed this wonderful book.

PHILIPPA PERRY

Contents

Lot 10

School Days

Kith and Kin

Afterwards

WARRIOR DAYS

My life was a series of battles, like those in European history that I studied without real understanding in the Royal Readers of my Guyana schooldays. After one war came another, without intermission, some of them long, hundred-year wars, and others short and bloody, but always conflict, never time to take your eye off the enemy, known or unknown.

These were women's battles, grand theaters of silence and sound; rarely were fathers involved. The role of the man as

9

breadwinner was to depart on bicycle early in the morning, return at noon when a hot meal, the main meal of the day, called breakfast, would be set before him. Then he would depart again and return at sunset, a day's work done.

Early on, I was inducted into its rituals. I became adept at the action of turning your back, of flouncing away, the cut eye, the suck teeth -- given double and triple application, the throwing of remarks, all these, preliminary to outright abuse. Sometimes sustained altercation came to a head in blows; like a bold period at the end of a sentence, it put an end to humbug and restored order.

Lot 10, First Street was the arena of this long protracted war, with sudden and lengthy seasons of strife. It was midway down the block, on the first street south of the Lamaha Canal.

The Lamaha Canal followed the trail of the Atlantic at ten feet below sea level. There is a wall of stone to keep out the sea but we knew its limitations; we had seen the ocean break through and menace our lives. Our houses were built high on stilts because in some rainy seasons, floods claimed our yards for many days.

When I compare my life as a child to what most people mean by neighborhood, I realize that we grew up in yards, not houses or even apartments. We were not sealed up in concrete with doors bolted, separate, and safe with sociability shut out. Nothing was hidden, you could see people at their open doors or windows living their lives, breathing their dreams aloud from morning till midnight; all round you the chattering, arguing, singing, laughing, and warring, with the radio on its single station blaring forth accompaniment.

The yard was a manor house microcosm; my relatives who owned the property lived in the large two-storied back house with two small apartments below and looked down, as it were, on two sets of paired cottages where we, and an assortment of tenants and poor relations, jostled each other to survive. An abundance of squabbling children in these households interacted across the spectrum from intense love to extreme enmity, and often was the root cause of many a conflict.

We were six children in our family cottage. Huddled in back between the alley and the breadfruit tree, the Jackson nine conducted their family rituals in conspiratorial secrecy. Nearby, were the seven Franklin children, the warrish Gorings, and the two beautiful Moore daughters among a ragtag bunch of brothers and animals. My mother's closest friend, Alma, became her bitter enemy after her daughter accused my sister of wearing a corset.

It is the noise I remember most, the feeling of invasion as soon as the sun rose. The throwing of remarks would begin at daybreak. When the humans paused for breath, there were sounds of animals: the squawking of chickens that every family prized, and the yelping of dogs that belonged to no one in particular.

You did not allow the sun to rise and find you in bed; our mothers did not tolerate that, and would rouse us harshly with a shout or a blow.

"How do you expect to succeed today? You are lying in bed receiving the sloth cast off by everyone who is awake and about," my mother would say, righteous in her defense when she poked me with a broomstick.

"Wake up, now," she would demand, warding off all imagined evil with her broom.

I understood the seething resentment that my mother harbored, set amongst her husband's relatives, never free from their watchful eyes. The grudges that other tenants held simmered below the surface, easily triggered to explosion by a simple careless remark or thoughtless act. My mother gossiped and we children played, but the terms of each fragile truce were clearly understood.

They hated us because we were the grandchildren of the owners and did not have to pay rent. These neighbors, who each week would ask for a few days grace, sometimes had to beg for credit. With their sour faced stares, they waited for us to stumble and fall. Goodwill was scarce; they waited for tragedy to strike.

The wooden cottage where we lived had three bedrooms, a kitchen with Dutch doors an extended hearth and small washroom, and a drawing room with paired Morris chairs, a desk and a souvenir chest where my mother could display the few precious things she owned.

My father, a trained carpenter and cabinetmaker, built most of our furniture. We had helped our parents weave the caning for the dining chairs, and we had filled the mattresses for our beds with coconut fiber and made our pillows too. In the girls bedroom there was my father's kit box from his soldier days in WWII, a black wooden trunk with his number 5776 on it, where we kept our particular clothes that were clean and ironed, safe in mothballs. My sister and I lined its cover with pictures of film stars that we cut from Photoplay magazines.

On the walls in my parent's bedroom hung two framed photographs, stills from their favorite movies: Fred Astaire and Ginger Rogers. The baby's crib stayed in their room, its legs standing in four small tins of water so that the ants that plague us continually would not get at her, and after she is weaned, she will come to sleep in the girl's bedroom, while the two boys sleep on a bunk bed in the tiny back room.

When I was little, I remember that I slept at night in my father's old army socks to keep my feet safe from mice that love to nibble the soles and palms of babies.

Only in the dead of night was there silence; but the night had its own terrors. We did not fear robbers – men who greased their skins and went out naked except for a tiny black buckta, they blended into the dark and slipped into houses. You could never catch them—they ran on their bare feet like cats and slipped through your fingers if you tried to grab them. They were after money and jewels – those thick gold bangles and corded chains of Mazaruni gold, passed down from grandmothers to mothers and hidden for maturing daughters.

We felt safe because there were so many people to raise hell if a thief ventured into our yard.

What we feared was the dead; the spirits that came out at night, the jumbies who roamed, the evil that was left unredeemed in our lives.

Everywhere some spirit broods, misfortune waits. God watches over his world, but the Evil Eye is watching too.

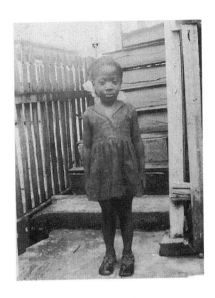

RING PLAY

During full moon, in the evenings, we children, clasped hands in the moonlight, pounding feet on the soft clay earth whirling round and round.

"Pussy in the moonlight
Pussy in the dew
Pussy never come back
Till half past two."

I grasp my older sister's hand, happy to be included with the bigger children, excited that the moon makes a mockery of nighttime and we can stay outdoors. Great vultures, carrion crows, swoop and land in far off coconut trees, the smell of ripe sapodillas rouse squealing night insects, the six o'clock beetle hisses, frogs whistle and splutter in dense hibiscus hedges, and raucous shouts of children pierce the air. Other children lured by the sounds of play, hordes of children, Pied Piper children skipping and leaping, stream into the moonlit yard. Silently, hands are joined, links in the ritual.

"Ring a ring a rosie, pocket full o'posie ..."

Stick legs of skinny brown children cross and re-cross in the round. Bare feet pound a faster rhythm on the bald clay earth, the game changes.

"Jumbie lef' he pipe here?" and the response, as fingers lock tighter, barring him out. "No, ko loko!"

The child outside the ring puts his entire weight on the locked hands, straining to break the bonds and enter the circle. Inside, the prize, another child, crouches then darts here and there away from the fingers reaching inside to grab at her. We shriek, we shout, I laugh until tears come. Voices rise to a crescendo,

"No, ko loko!"

But the link breaks, the jumbie crosses the circle, children scatter in all directions, shrieking loudly. We have to form the circle and start all over again.

A few mothers look out from the aprons of their doors.

"Go away from my door mouth!"

"No ring play at my door!"

"Go away!" our mothers cry, "Enough ring play for one day."

Ring play brings bad luck they say. That is what they also have against "littie", the game we play with five smooth little stones.

"No littie on my stoop," they say, "littie brings bad luck."

Everywhere some spirit broods, misfortune waits. God watches over his world, but the Evil Eye is watching too. Wear red for protection; we wear red ribbons in our braided hair.

We move to neutral ground. A stray dog licks himself lazily, and slinks out of our way. I remember how we formed again, linking hands as if we were forced to continue our game, as if we were not yet done for that day.

"There's a brown girl in the ring, tra la la la ..." A lively one, but the concrete slab on which we dance is hard on the soles of our feet until we slow to a mournful ditty:

"Old Rogers was dead and he lay in his grave. Oye, oye, oye"

A slow spin to the left, a slow spin to the right. The moon slides behind the tall tree shadows, and I grip my sister's hand clutching at her fingers trying not to think of the words of the song. The concrete slab on which we dance is my great grandmother's grave. She died in childbirth and Sir Carrie, my great grandfather, buried the child with her on his property. Practical man that he was, he made the slab of concrete large and wide for other purposes, like bleaching laundry in the sun or drying trays of beans. Around it, scrub grass and wild flowers struggle to grow. We play until, perhaps, another mother chides or else we tire and slink behind our doors to sleep.

The next day, or could have been a few days after that, I wake to hear a neighbor's child has died. There is much activity among the adults. Food is cooked, covered dishes sent and returned empty, talk and whispers, and moans of regret. Nothing is explained to me so I walk around, invisible except for my ears. There will be no funeral. The family is poor, the child was not baptized. These people do not deal with doctors, let nature claim her own. I watch all morning from my window, marking every movement in our neighbor's house. Her window is open and I watch.

She is washing the dead baby in her kitchen sink in much the same way she washed him any other day. Her face swollen from crying, her hair covered, a flowered scarf tied round it, she holds the body slanted in the basin, her left hand steadied against the tap, and moves a cloth slowly over the brown limbs with her right. I stare in silent fascination. I never tell my mother what I saw.

Later, dressed in Sunday clothes, my sister and I are sent across the yard to pay our respects. My sister, older and more fearful because of all the tales of ghosts and death that she has heard on many more moonlit nights than I have seen, does not want to go. I am tingling with expectation. Did our ring play cause of the baby's death? No one has said it but somehow a connection forms in my mind and I am excited and frightened at the same time.

We enter the cottage, the grandmother leads us to the room where the child lies on a bed and the mother with swollen eyes sits numbly in a chair. The baby wears white, a shirt or nightshirt, stark white against his straight brown limbs. His skin is shiny like polished mahogany and the smell of bay leaves is everywhere. As I stare at the child, my eyes focus on his eyes, on the coins that cover his eyes. Copper coins, brown and shiny as his face, old copper coins smooth with use and blackened brown, King George on one side and Britannia with her trident and chariot ruling the waves on the other side.

I got pennies every Saturday as my allowance. Sometimes I saved them; sometimes I bought candy. I always spent the old ones first.

BREAD AND COAL

I am with my hatchet making chips for the coal-pot in the dusk of the tropics of my childhood.

I know well to avoid pitch pine, a wood that smokes and blackens all our pots and gives such little heat and fuel that water does not boil for tea and my mother, angry at yet one more disappointment, frets and scolds.

My sister is nine and I am six and after school , before we play, we sweep the fire hearth clean of ashes and bring out chunks of wallaba logs, and greenheart, boxwood and lightwood, womora and white pine. We take the short handled hatchet, its blade sharp and dangerous but we are careful and we sit and take our time; we will do a good job of making kindling, we will not hurry and cut thumbs or get splinters underneath our nails because we are in such a haste to play. We will be careful as our mother has taught us, and afterwards we shred clean coconut fiber and make a paste of sand and ashes to scour the iron pots we use for cooking.

The world of work was natural, nothing came easy, and the smallest comfort came at the end of a long laborious process. It took our mothers all day, from daybreak to dusk, to gather food from markets and put the main noon meal, called breakfast, and morning and evening tea upon the table, to keep the house clean and the clothes washed and mended. The only saving grace was that during all this work my mother socialized unhurriedly with her neighbors; they chatted, they gossiped, they quarreled, they visited; they let their lives flow as their time was eaten up in the trivia of survival.

My mother was the first woman in the yard to get a two-burner oil stove. Kerosene transformed my life. My commerce with wood chips and ashes ended; the pots were cleaner now except for rare accidents when the burners flared up. My sister and I now had a few more hours of play.

It had all come to a head that Christmas when my mother had planned to bake her Christmas black cake at the same time that she baked the family's weekly bread. For this we used a box oven that my father had built and which performed pretty well once you used good coals.

On Friday afternoon, my sister and I would buy coals from the Wilsons who lived down our street. A little wooden bridge across a ditch separated their house from the street, but they were a people apart from the rest of us. They were Jordanites, a sect of Seventh Day Adventists who shut up their shop for worship on their Saturday Sabbath.

The Wilsons lived in a two-room arrangement, though there must have been at least six people in the family; the front room was their coal shop and their private life transpired behind a blackened curtain.

The entire family was blackened by their trade. Only on Saturdays, dressed in white and led by Mr. Wilson with his donkey cart as they set out for their church, did the neighbors recognize that the Wilson girls were light brown skinned and pretty. Washed of all the soot and grime, they looked radiant, white kerchiefs covered their heads and their modestly long-sleeved dresses came to their ankles.

Their father strode before them, his matted hair long and uncombed, his beard flowing and his loose white garments swirling about his bare legs, his feet in unaccustomed brown shoes. We thought he looked like Moses, the patriarch in our Aunt's Illustrated Bible

When my mother had laid out her bread in rolls after the second rising and covered them with a tea towel, she mixed her cake and prepared the box oven for baking. It stood under our house, about the size of a medium refrigerator, a wooden box lined with tin, galvanized iron or some such material. There were two shelves in it and in the bottom, the coal pot stoked with good black coal. The door latched with a wooden clasp and my mother would place dampened jute bags around the door seal over the top of the oven. She claimed that this was to moderate the heat and refine the baking process. Every now and then, she would remove the jute bags, soak them again and drape them over the oven.

She depended on her sense of smell to know when the bread was ready, or when the cake needed to be tested, and most times, she had the accuracy of a scientist at this task. When the baked bread was set out to cool on our kitchen table, the entire yard could smell the enticing aroma. There was nothing more delicious than a freshly baked roll, still warm from the oven with a great gob of butter swiftly melting inside.

On this particular occasion, something went horribly wrong. Great clouds of smoke wafted from the oven door and all the damping of jute bags were in vain. My mother opened the oven door and tried to retrieve her baking from the inferno.

"This is the last bread I will bake in this oven," she swore, her eyes red from the smoke and tears of frustration. We came near but the billowing smoke drove us back into the open yard. We started to fill buckets with water while my mother battled in her oven mitts salvaging sheets of blackened half-cooked dough. Afterwards, we tried to save some of the bread by brushing milk over their blackened surfaces and taking them over to a neighbor's oven, but my mother was inconsolable. She dumped the cake, pan and all, into the garbage and burst into loud sobs.

What kind of life was this? What was the point of even trying to do anything? She railed to no one in particular.

After a while, she became logical. Why had the oven that had always served her well in other times malfunctioned? It was the coals. It was Mr. Wilson cheating; poor coals, half-burned wood, the smell of pitch pine!

Never again, she swore and she cursed the Wilsons for their thievery, their hypocritical religion, their filthy sooty lives and their ridiculous white robes. She could hardly complain to them directly; it was Saturday and the Wilsons, transformed, were baptizing Jordanite converts on the banks of the Lamaha canal.

When my father bought the oil stove as my mother's Christmas present, he also bought the oven that fit on top of the stove for bread baking days. For a time my mother was appeased.

CHINA

My mother made a vow that morning in the rain that the first money I ever earned would have to pay her back for this trial I was putting her through. She stood at the open doorway with the rain pelting down as if God himself wept in agreement with her, wringing her hands at the destruction of the one good thing left from her marriage.

She made it seem as if I, the destroyer, with the fire of spite in my eyes, had taken a sledgehammer and struck down the last good thing in her blighted life, but really, it was not like that at all.

I can still hear her shriek and scream like a wounded animal, rousing the neighbors to stand at their door mouths gaping, and winning them over to her side. Our yard was the theater of my childhood; my mother the tragic heroine. In the property owned by her in-laws, she was always the outsider, the striver, the one who did not really belong among them. I see them as the rabble at an execution, arms waving, faces contorted, soundless in the rain of their hate.

You cannot hate a child of seven. Even God does not record the sins of one so young. It is an error, an aberration; I will wake up in the sunlight and find it was a dream that never happened. I am exaggerating, you say, making high drama out

25

I can emphatize

of a simple story. Only on the surface, it seems simple; otherwise, it would not pain me so many years later to tell it.

Every day I had chores in the bathroom, which in our house, was a room for more than taking a shower. It was a large wooden stall reinforced with zinc reaching halfway up around a slab of concrete floor. There was a drain in the center of the floor and a shower spout above. Light came in from the upper space between the wall and ceiling. A few hooks behind the door were for towels and a corner shelf held soaps and calabashes; below this shelf was the area for chamber pots waiting to be washed. We had no indoor toilet. The slop buckets and potties for each bedroom were made of enamel, but the pride of my mother's room was a porcelain china chamber pot with a washbasin and ewer to match. The ewer sat in the basin on her washstand, a solid piece of mahogany furniture with roller towel racks on the sides and a shelf below with a hole to fit the chamber pot. This pot with the blue forget-me-nots under a pink border was a decoration, to be dusted and admired for years, I thought, for dusting was my Saturday chore. How did it come to be in the shower stall?

All of a sudden, it began appearing among the other pots in the corner of the bathroom. And, it contained blood! The first time I was startled. I washed the other pots and did not touch it. Later on, it disappeared. Another time it contained bloody water, a rag soaking in bloody water. Where did the blood come from? Who was bleeding to death? If only my mother knew the agony of my imaginings! I could not guess the origin of her wounds but I was sure that my mother was going to die. I looked at the blood, touched it, smelled it.

One day I decided that the blood seemed diluted and weak, so I reassured myself that my mother was recovering. I was too young to know, no one had ever told me, and, in a culture where children are expected to be seen and not heard, I did not ask. It was my own investigation and my overwhelming dread that broke the chamber pot. I screamed as the bloody mess surged and swamped and the shards of china fell away on the concrete floor. I cut my hand, somehow, and now there was my own blood in it, but I did not feel pain, my terror of meddling into what was not my business and my fear of my mother's wrath consumed me.

I looked up to see her at the bathroom door.

Why did you touch it?

This was not my mother whose impending death had so terrified me. She was a large looming stranger whose shouts and screams mingled with my own wild cries.

I stood fearful and naked among the battered enamel buckets, trying to avoid the sharp shards of broken china flowers. Cowering against the walls, knocking over other noisy pots, I nodded my head, agreed that I was too curious for my own good, and with tears and mucous streaming from my face, my scrawny body heaved with sobs of distress.

I set about gathering up the pieces; the base was still intact, but it was hopeless to even think of gluing it all back together. So, with the pieces gathered into the base, blood from my hand smearing everything, I was led out. She made me walk naked, out of the bathroom, through the kitchen, out our back door, into the yard.

The neighbors were watching at their doors. Their children, my own playmates in happier times, now giggled and snickered, and were laughing at me. As the rain beat down on my shivering body, there was mockery all around me but I did not look at any face, I did not search out any eyes. I believe that I had stopped my own crying and fixed my gaze defiantly on a single broken bouquet of forget-me-nots. Perhaps the truth is that I registered blank, erased the minutes it took to walk in the rain from the base of our stoop through the entire length of the sodden clay and gravel yard to the dumping ground in back, where broken glass and damaged bits and pieces were stored for making concrete.

On another level, this event was hardly diabolical. It was a frequent happening in our yard, that when it rained, children would run out and play, some naked, some with only underpants. This was no play today, I was the one sent out and the vultures had gathered to watch.

I did not hear their jeers; I blocked them all out. But my eyes could not shut out their stares and their grimaces.

The rain and the sound of the rain became my comfort. I could hear its vicious slamming against our zinc roofs, its torrent, the anger I was unable to express. When it slowed to a rumble and gentle hiss, I plotted sly retribution.

I would grow up. I would leave this place that scorned me and never return. I would send back, anonymously, dozens of chamber pots. Every year, on this day in March, I would mail to my mother, who will not know my whereabouts, a decorated china potty.

What motivation?

SEVEN

I was exactly in the year of freedom. After age seven, my grandmother and old aunts had informed me, my mistakes would no longer be forgiven, and the scorekeeper in the sky would begin chalking up my doom. I was on edge that year, practicing my actions and my understandings of the world so that I would do right, and choose the path that did not lead to sinning, so that I would chalk up credits for good works that would balance against mistakes that in my clumsiness I was sure to commit.

One method that I perfected was listening to the old people, walking with them and watching, tagging along beside my mother, clinging to her until she brushed me aside in annoyance:

I was a thorn in her side, a leech so that she could not express herself when she saw her friends and wanted to gossip, I was a busybody who heard everything and asked too many questions. *bond between mother a child*

My Aunt Cil who was a spinster, enjoyed my company and took one or two of us children with her wherever she went. To church, on walks, to tea parties, to visit her friends, even the sick ones, to the cinema on holidays, to band concerts on the sea wall. The only place we did not accompany Aunt Cil was to funerals-- at that my mother drew the line. My Aunt attended at least one or two funerals a week, whether or not she was a close friend of the deceased. She did not attend wakes if she could help, because the hymn singing ceded too quickly to carousing and rum drinking, she said.

Aunt Cil said that people like Miss Williams were to be pitied. On a day when they least expect it, the circulation of the blood will stop because fat will cover the heart. I imagined swirls of fat, dense and gray on the surface of my mother's Sunday soup before she skimmed it off, but there had to be more of it, surging thick and brown like the Demerara River foaming up against the sea wall and poor Miss Williams dumbfounded, struggling to escape.

Miss Williams had an only son, a police constable, stationed at Kwakwani, in the North West. There was always some squabbling over territory there; if our police were not vigilant Venezuela would steal our mountains and minerals, Brazil would gobble up our vast cattle plains, and the poor Guyanese people would be left marooned on the narrow strip of coast land with a few grains of rice and straggling sticks of sugar cane.

I understood, even at my young age, how important Miss Williams' son was to my future, and what a great sacrifice his mother was making, like the gold-star mothers in American movies who sent their only sons to war. She was given no stars whatever; she toiled alone in her ground provision shop under her house. I respected Miss Williams even though she smelt funny, when I went to her bottom house to buy vegetables for metagee and for our Sunday soup.

31

Two pounds of yam, two pound cassava, eddoes, one dasheen, a small hand of yellow plantains and one of green, I would read from my mother's list, after I had greeted Miss Williams and asked after her health as I was properly brought up to do.

Then I would watch as she slowly moved over to the great mountains of jute bags that contained the produce, rotate her body with great effort, bend down so that her flowered house dress swept the floor, and laboriously haul out huge black tentacles of cassava.

"My mother said to send the good, floury cassava like you did two weeks ago, " I said boldly, and when she looked up to cut her eyes at me, I continued quickly, trying to convince her that I was not being womanish or rude, because my mother had really made that statement.

"Last week the cassava you sent was hard and waxy."

Miss Williams sucked her teeth as she ambled over to her scale that was set up on a narrow counter.

"Child," she said, with a weariness meant to insult me, "Tell your mother they don't give me a chance to examine every stick of cassava before they put it in the bag and sell it to me."

She was piling up my order at the corner of the counter, and it was dark and a bit warm in the shop, the only light and air coming from a single jalousie window and the open door.

She moved to the plantains, that stood upright in a tall tangle of green and yellowing, and I started to wonder at my mother's direction: a small hand of green plantain, whose hand? Not my small hand, certainly. Miss Williams knew what she meant and did not bat an eyelash. She started to hum a tune, unruffled by my hopping from one foot to the other, in my impatience to go out and play. With calm and deliberate slowness, she put together the entire market order as she had been doing for so many years for all the mothers of Lot 10.

I looked at her placid face, flat and pale yellow-brown like the incarnation of the moon. Her cheeks ended in squarish jowls, and she had almost no neck, but from the back, her beautiful head of straight black hair cascaded down to her middle.

She was a bovianda, part black and part buck, which was how we referred to aboriginal Indians. I knew she was not a Carib, because as we had learned in our West Indian Readers, Columbus had wiped them all out in his discovery of the New World; she might have been a Wai-Wai or Wapisiano, one of the friendlier tribes.

Aunt Cil said that it was her good disposition that kept her healthy. God had blessed her with a contented mind.

I asked my aunt why Miss Williams smelled so unlike anyone else, and my aunt replied that it was perhaps the coconut oil in her hair. I did not exactly believe this because I knew well the sweet, rancid smell of coconut oil, and the odor trapped under Miss Williams' bottom house market was something quite different. I pondered as I watched her, and decided that it was poor personal hygiene -- it was hard when washing for someone her size to find their way into all the creases and folds of her body.

Miss Williams lived with a tall, thin black man, who came and went about his business delivering her supplies and taking frequent stints in the bush to pan for gold. When he was around she referred to him as "he", not by name, and he had very little to say for himself; he only smiled a lot showing numerous gold teeth.

"He brought me two cases of very sweet grapefruit from Pomeroon," Miss Williams would boast, sharing her bounty with the neighbors, or "Try this avocado, he brought a box of these and all ripening at the same time."

She would share also the bad news he brought from the interior, sighing and rolling her eyes in distress, "He say, dengue fever raging in Bartica!"

Sometimes she would shut up her shop when he was in town and the neighbors would laugh and make jokes about Miss Williams' second honeymoon. However, most of the time she was a hard-working woman, weighing her provisions and carefully counting up her money.

On the radio at nights, death announcements came after the nine o'clock news, and everyone kept their radios on up to that time, then shut off everything and hustled children to bed.

Just about that time one night we heard this loud wailing. It was not the usual domestic uproar, the thump, the wail, the silence. This was loud, sad, and uncontrollable wailing and moaning. Everyone streamed from the cottages to see what was wrong.

"It is Miss Williams' son," someone said. "Killed!"

"Oh God, trouble on the border," someone else amended in alarm.

"How did you hear?"

It came over the radio.

"Are you sure? How could they announce it and nobody come to inform his mother first," said Aunt Cil with implacable logic. But nobody bothered to follow up her comment because Miss Goring, a busybody from down the street, said loud and clear:

"Yes, I heard the name. Cecil Burgess Williams. Yes, I heard it distinctly. I heard the announcer say it."

Pursing her lips, she led the charge into Miss Williams' house.

Miss Williams was rolling on her floor, her husband trying vainly with his thin arms to hold and comfort her. My mother got busy at once with the other women, picking Miss Williams huge body off the floor, applying smelling salts to her nose; they were too engrossed to heed the children who came to the open door to stare.

I was amazed that Miss Williams who was always so much in control in her shop could behave with such wild abandon. She was banging her head against the floor; her hair disheveled streaming in a tangled mass, her clothes in disarray exposing her flesh. With each upward swoop, she would pound her fists and rattle her heels in a fast, agitated rhythm. It was as if her great frame possessed superhuman energy, as if her large limbs became so weightless that she could throw them off in her grief.

The women came close and put damp towels against her brow. Aunt Cil was convinced that the next event would be a seizure so she kept urging for calm:

"Quiet", she said," Trust God. Think of your heart, don't upset yourself."

Miss Williams' husband went off to the local police station in Albert Street to find out particulars about her son's death, and the women took over and started to cook food for the wake. Bottles of rum appeared and people began setting up Miss Williams' front room. They succeeded in getting her off the floor and led her into the bedroom. Two women sat with her, the others in the kitchen got the pots going.

Someone remembered that children should be in bed because the next day was a school day, but nobody really cared, nobody shooed us away, and I stayed put until her husband returned.

It turned out that it was not her son at all, but an older man with the same name in a completely different part of the country. Yes, he was sure, because at the station, they were able to contact her son's division in the northwest, and everything there was fine.

Miss Williams started to weep and wail again, she wanted to see her son for herself or at least to hear his voice. She kept on weeping, gasping and having palpitations. She needed the smelling salts and the women's arms to lean on and it began to look dangerous for her heart.

It took her several weeks to recover and the shop under her house remained dark and shut. My mother said the rats were having sport with Miss Williams' rotting provisions under her house, and I had to go to the next street to buy produce from Miss Boodhoo, a sour tempered woman who everybody knew was an old haigue.

When Miss Williams' shop finally opened again, she had shrunk to half her former size. She was glad to be smaller she said, it was so much easier on the heart.

RADIO DAYS

"Coming to you on Zed F Y, every Tuesday night at seven-thirty, it's the Ovaltine Hour."

In a country where the streetlights were shut off at ten and television had not yet arrived, ZFY, the single radio station could count on the undivided attention of everyone within the beam of its waves.

In the morning, on waking people turned radios on and left them on until they went to bed: Indian religious music at 5AM, BBC news at 7:15 -- AM and PM -- popular songs all day, birthday requests and death announcements, all flowed about their ears as the leitmotif of their lives.

My sisters and I knew all the words of all the songs they played, and at night we thrilled with terror as Mystery Theatre and the Black Museum came on. Our greatest wish, however, was to be chosen for the Ovaltine Hour.

We did not question that we were talented -- our parents, neighbors, and relatives were always generous with their praise whenever we performed for them. They praised me for remembering long verses from the Bible, and my sister's voice stood out whenever we sang together.

The Ovaltine Hour was a children's talent show, rewarding precocity and surprise. Piano and violin prodigies had a higher chance of selection if they chose pieces with flourish and style. Mimics and verse speakers were rewarded for humor and expressiveness.

When I was seven and my sister ten, our cousin Aubrey listened to us practice, and then took us to audition one Saturday afternoon.

We were very excited because Aubrey had taken part in the adult contest and had made the cut to sing on the radio quite a few times. Everyone said he was a natural, just needed professional training, and though he had always missed the grand prize, the family had enjoyed his consolation prize of Malt Extract.

When we got to the audition hall, we saw children in little clusters practicing their songs and recitations, with their mothers eagerly trying to attract the attention of the station employees, assuming anyone official looking was a talent scout. Aubrey marched us past the waiting parents, saying that we were going directly to Mr. Vivian Lee, the Master of Ceremonies with whom he was familiar.

The secretary at the desk said that, unfortunately, Mr. Lee was not in, and l began to fear that we would be lost among the eager children outside. Aubrey, undeterred, sat us down and began to joke around with the secretary. Then she left and he began to give us "pointers".

"Just do exactly what I tell you, when l tell you," he said, then looking especially at me, "and you, don't contradict anything I say!"

He then began to rehearse my sister, the singer, and Pam started up:

"My Bonnie lies over the ocean..."

Mr. Lee emerged from inside and greeted Aubrey. My sister continued to sing:

"My Bonnie lies over the sea..."

Mr. Lee raised his hand to silence her:

"She's got a good, strong voice all right."

"These are my nieces," said Aubrey, "and little Pamie here is not shy."

Aubrey nodded to her, and her voice rose in the chorus:

"Bring back, bring back, o' bring back my bonnie to me, to me , to me…"

She was so loud that other people approached the door to look in.

"She's good," Mr. Lee observed laughing," She doesn't even need a mike! "

Aubrey knew she was in.

"June is good too," Aubrey persisted pushing me forward, "and she is only five."

I stopped in surprise at this blatant lie. I was sure that Mr. Lee was no fool, so if Aubrey had to shrink my age to squeeze me through, he must not be too confident about my talent. So my confidence buckled too.

"Go ahead, "he encouraged.

I felt confused and two lines into my smart poem about "Mr. Homer of Crumble Corner", I could feel that Mr. Lee was not listening and I began to mumble.

"We got too many recitations," he told Aubrey, "Let them try duets", he suggested, "she could sing with her sister next time."

Aubrey had to be satisfied with that because Mr. Lee was a very busy man and, after all, Pam was in!

The secretary wrote the particulars down and Pam joined a smaller group of children in another room practicing in front of the microphone. I felt useless though l was happy for my sister.

My radio days were over; we would never sing duets because my mother always said l couldn't carry a tune to save my life.

We made a party on the night of Pam's radio debut. The relatives had gathered and everyone had brought an item of food to put on the kitchen table.

Everyone went to the drawing room and took their places for the show. My mother set out drinks and fancy biscuits on a tray and brought it out just as the Ovaltine theme song came on. The radio volume was up to the maximum and our neighbors, forewarned, all had their radios blaring forth.

In spite of this riotous din, the relatives in our house insisted on carrying on conversations.

We had no idea of the order of the performances, so we had to stop chattering to hear what was coming up next, and between each of the items, came the word from our sponsor.

Nobody thought to turn the volume down at these times, no one wanted to risk missing Pam when she came on, so everyone talked loudly above the radio and everyone talked at the same time.

"She's coming up now," my Uncle Fred ventured when there was a pause.

"Did you hear them announce it?" my mother asked, anxious that she had missed something. She had been commenting on a humorous poem that had just been rendered by one of the regulars -- a smart child, Caroline Pierce -- saying that it was time to let others, meaning me, her daughter, have a chance on the show.

"Yes, she's coming now, " another uncle persisted, during the health tip from Ovaltine, "they just had an instrumental and then a recitation, they've got to have a song next."

 That sounded reasonable enough since Uncle Phil was a radio expert of sorts. He played guitar in a trio that accompanied the Zex Soap half- hour show on Monday nights. They did the intro number, an intermission piece, and the windup. Fame eluded him because they never introduced the players by name – they called the three men simply, the Zex Soap Trio.

"A song, yes, "Aunt Ella agreed, "but how do you know it is Pamie's song?"

They were just getting into a discussion about logic, when the sounds of "My Bonnie " flooded the room. Everyone yelled "shhhhh ,shhhhhh"

The second verse was going before we had the appropriate silence to enjoy Pam's performance.

At the end, everyone clapped, and then they all wanted to hear her sing the whole song so we never heard the rest of the radio show.

The judge awarded the grand prize to a ten year old who had played a complicated classical piece on the piano, and that started another argument in our drawing room.

Aunt Ella said that violins and piano were necessary for culture and my father wanted to know whose culture she was talking about.

In the end, they agreed that it was fair to encourage children who needed to practice many hours and whose parents had to pay for expensive music lessons.

l began to wonder if could have a chance at fame by playing a musical instrument, but except for my uncle`s guitar in our house I had never come close to another musical instrument and the possibility seemed remote.

l put away those thoughts as we ended our evening with a cup of Ovaltine, my sister`s consolation prize.

A few years later, I redeemed myself on the radio by winning a case of Wheat Sheaf Evaporated Milk for submitting a question to the show "Stump the Panel"....Guess Who, Guess Where, Guess What ?

I stumped them with my clue "Ask Bill?" Answer: "William Tell".

THE YELLOW FEVER MAN

Aunt Sybil fell in love with the yellow fever man. He used to come twice a month in his civil service cork hat, khaki shorts and matching knee socks balancing his scientific equipment in a small wooden box on the handle of his bicycle.

His black leather shoes were always shine, even after it rained and he had stood in mud in front of our vat to check for mosquitoes and germs. We would go outside and stand near him as he sifted, measured and examined, and our mother would appear at the open flap of our back door and call out:

"Come inside, come inside…don't disturb the gentleman, let him do his work, don't get in his way!"

We were curious children and we clustered about him. I wondered how he could see if germs were in there and I would come close, right under his elbow, not even caring about the little green and black frogs that scattered madly when he began to collect up water in his little bottles. Every now and then, he would look at the silver watch on his wrist, and he would take little colored pellets from the pouch at his belt and put them in the bottles before tightening their corks and putting them away.

"Is that candy?" Victor asked one day, and the man put his pellets away and said:

"No, my son, this is science!"

When we asked about science and the yellow fever man, my grandmother corrected us:

"He is a sanitary inspector and he had to study and pass a lot of exams to get that job. If you stop playing so much and study your school work, that's what you could grow up to be!"

When he was done with his examination of the vat, he walked over to the standpipe where mothers bathed small children, then to the drain that ran down the length of the yard into the alley out back. He wrote out and signed a certificate that he brought it to my grandmother's door, since she was the property owner.

This was when Aunt Sybil got her chance. She would be waiting for him with smiles and sometimes lemonade. Sybil pretended to be shy and looked at the man with adoration, telling us to be quiet when we called him "bandy-legged.'

My grandmother sucked her teeth and said she was wasting her time because a man with such a good job was surely married already or at least had some woman and children hanging on to him.

I do not recall that we ever knew his name, but we knew that his work was protecting us from the myriad diseases that struck children all over the world. We knew that the tiny mosquitoes that we slapped against our legs were carriers of malaria, filaria and yellow fever, and though we joked about sleeping sickness when we wanted to stay in bed, we were well aware that tinier insects and all sorts of flies had wiped out whole villages in Africa.

In the rainy season, anything left outdoors got damp and moldy, and the sun could not shine long enough to dry things out and make us cheerful again. So we sat indoors in boredom, pulled the wings off rain flies and watched as lizards slunk their way up the walls and onto the ceiling changing their colors from dirty brown to dirty milky white.

We had to stay indoors and keep our feet dry so we would not catch cold or chills, which led to shaking bouts of ague.

If the rain persisted and the drains overflowed, the yard was flooded and we knew we were in for the most dangerous mosquito season. The men dug new drains and we all pitched in to empty any cans where stagnant water would make a breeding ground.

When I think of what disease prevention meant in the climate of my childhood, I recognize how hard it was for parents to keep their children alive. We made an effort at hygiene but the conditions did not encourage success.

We tried to protect our food from flies, we washed our hands particularly after bathroom use, but not everyone had running water indoors and none of the houses had screens on windows or doors.

Stray animals were everywhere, fed by everyone though belonging to no one, and the openness of our lives meant that everyone was exposed and everything spread.

Our parents countered with herbal preventatives and bush remedies. Everyone grew and tended aloes, soldier's parsley and painkiller bush and prescribed them for a host of maladies. Cascara root we boiled and tempered its bitterness with muscatel wine; we were fed a large tablespoon of this before bedtime to keep our blood pure and our skin clean, without any thought of the alcohol effect on children.

Our daily ritual after bathing was to rub our limbs with a mixture of crab oil and coal tar, and at the first sign of a sore, my mother applied sulfur powder mixed with Vaseline. We were lucky that we did not suffer from yaws and thrush caused by the ubiquitous yard dust.

No amount of sweeping and sprinkling could subdue the acrid curtain of dust that the wind swirled into our eyes and nostrils; we would get a short respite after a sudden rain but a dusty film covered everything.

I learned early to detect and dislike the flavor of senna pods and senna leaves that my mother boiled and sweetened and passed off as tea. It was supposed to cure a variety of ailments connected with the liver and the blood.

Before the start of every school term , we were fed a dose of castor oil as a general all-purpose internal cleanser. We took castor oil on Sunday and fasted for the remainder of the day. By Monday morning, we were ready. A good start meant a good start everywhere!

Every child I knew had had a bout with measles, mumps and whooping cough. Some might have a bad case and suffer many weeks, but most of us managed to survive. At least three of the children on our street had died from these seemingly common illnesses. What started as a familiar ailment changed to something else or affected another part of the body, and by the time their parents called a doctor or rushed them to hospital, it was too late.

The coffins for children were white, we wore our Sunday school dresses and carried bunches of fragrant oleander.

We grew up knowing the thin line between life and death, even better than the one between illness and health. Red flannel tied around your neck, red ribbons in your hair, any protection from evil and any hope for deliverance, we grasped at eagerly.

The yellow fever man, the school nurse, and the health visitor who came into our yards for a new baby, were our links with the medical system. After my baby days, I never saw a doctor nor had my temperature taken with a thermometer until I was ten years old.

If I had a fever, my mother could tell how bad it was by touching my forehead; she swabbed me and bundled me up with Limacol, brewed daisy tea and put me to bed. Camphor, eucalyptus and bay leaves until now evoke in me a sense of comfort and ease.

At primary school, the public health campaigns began. One week in the late 1950s, they gave a tuberculosis test to all the children; each class queued up to be pricked by the nurse. We were not to scratch with our fingernails, nor get the bruise wet. Nothing on my forearm, mine was negative so I got the painful vaccination on my upper arm that gave me a fever, left a sore for months, and a scar like a flower, forever.

In primary school, we learned the rules for good and healthy living from inscriptions on the walls of our classroom and we wrote them out as penmanship practice: Cleanliness is next to godliness. Wash your hands before every meal. Clean and brush your teeth at least twice a day.

We learned the life cycles of flies, and grew to hate them as they moved from the waste of stray animals in our yards and then lighted on our table. We drew pictures and studied the features of the mosquitoes that scourged the tropics.

The anopheles mosquito carried malaria and we were lucky that there had not been an epidemic for a long time; the culex mosquito that carried filaria was more devious because my grandmother Dada had filaria that flared up only at certain times, swelled her legs and laid her out for days with raging fever. Typhoid we knew, but we had never seen the devastation of yellow fever.

In 1955, the government decreed the destruction of all vats since they were the main cause of water borne epidemics. Vats collected rainwater, and some were great monstrous wooden structures bigger and taller than houses with roof gutters feeding into them. They had sieves at the top and a spout and tap near the bottom where people drew their drinking water.

Sometimes a cat would be missing for days only to turn up drowned in the vat from which people continued to draw water. Birds and bats flew from the sapodilla tree and lodged droppings nearby. Water frogs were always welcome, but how many of these tiny frogs could keep so many gallons of water pure.

My grandmother was very upset, there was nothing like fresh rainwater, she said. We kept our vat in good repair and every day my grandmother filled her earthenware goblet and placed its silver cup beside it on a tray in her portico.

It was a sad day when our vat was broken down, but what a horrible mess it hid; it looked and smelled like the repository of all the strays that had ever disappeared. The spot with scattered concrete blocks that formed the base of the vat remained damp and slimy for a long time afterward and was the evening gathering place for toads; perhaps, because they missed the vat they croaked loud disapproval.

My grandmother rented a small bottom house apartment to a widower from one of the small islands. She could not recall if he said he was from Dominica and his late wife from St. Kitts or if the attribution was the other way round. In any case, he was a "highlander" as far as the neighbors were concerned, a man with habits foreign to their own.

Of particular concern was his love for frogs and toads. He delighted in the population that gathered in the vat space at sundown, and encouraged them by sitting out with a pot of boiled white rice and dealing out handfuls for them. He would make clucking noises and refer to the creatures by names as if he were training a host of new pets.

We would come out and watch while he lifted a toad, hefted it, and put it back down among its fellows. Then the frogs would slither away and Mr. Owen would go back into his apartment to read his Bible.

"Frogs are a delicacy", he said, "We call them mountain chicken." We were, none of us, ever brave enough to taste his food.

With our vat gone, we soon became accustomed to huge steel drums set out at night to catch rainwater, and after boiling, we filled the red earthenware goblet and let it chill to a welcome drink of water that we hoped was safe.

Nothing ever happened between Aunt Sybil and the yellow fever man. She went through her courting phase and eventually became engaged to Vibert, a photographer whose mother was my grandmother's friend. We children made sport by spying on the lovers as they kissed goodnight near the spot where the old vat used to be.

YAWARI

It made Dora's skin crawl to see that corded tail, like a whip with a mind of its own, the tiny chisels of its teeth and those deceitful eyes. It was an old person's face, a devil face with the sly knowing smile, mocking her life. You're not going to escape or amount to anything, I know, I know so well...mocking her struggle to better herself, belittling the small things she was so careful to do to set herself apart from her husband's family, ringed around her in their little cottages all in the same yard.

With vicious determination, she put on Phil's guard boots, an old pair without laces that she could slip her foot into easily with the heavy house socks she was wearing. She shouted to Evelyn and Sylvie who came out of their cottages ready, with brooms and long sticks and wearing boots- they did not want the animal scurrying over their toes either. Like a hunting party, in concentrated formation, they crawled under the house among the chicken coops and broken down pens of boxwood and wire mesh lashed together with bits of chain or rope. The smell of diluted disinfectant, Jeyes fluid that they bought in brown beer bottles, now in milky pools around the coops, could not mask the sweet acrid stench of layers and layers of bird droppings and damp chicken feathers.

To the left of the coops, an area in shadow had two large trunks, the kind that people took on long sea voyages or luxury cruises ages ago, with bolts in its corners and bindings. These contained Dora's legacy, her mother's valuables brought here in a dray cart for safekeeping when the old woman was put out of her home. Dora had rescued some of the more useful pieces; an amazing lot of china when she opened it, some wrapped in cloths, delicate with exquisite patterns , many cracked and chipped, saved from various places her mother had worked as a parlor maid. Not wanting to be reminded of her mother's troubles, she had put the crates away in the corner of the bottom house.

A box of books stood near them, careless and overflowing, old textbooks with stained covers, Royal Readers that had got wet then had harbored cockroaches. Now in the damp, fetid air of the bottom house who knows what strange creatures lurked.

This looked like a good spot, this was the place to set up operations; they were sure that the animal was here.

Phil was sure he had spied it, he said, on a beam, one of the heavy wallaba beams that supported the cottage on posts, over there, right above the boxes. He was sure he had seen a tail flash when he was taking his bike out that morning. He had to go to work, he had no time to ferret it out, perhaps tonight, he said, when he got in and settled down after his dinner. Dora knew this was just talk; maybe he was willing, but it made no sense. He would be gone to his other job as a security guard at night, and if not on duty, he would be off playing dominoes with his friends. This was women's business; the home and everything around it was the domain of the wife; so she knew she needed the other women to help.

Dora explained to the others:

"I could sense yawari. Every day I feeling this hen, and I feeling egg, and every day nothing. And this is not just one fowl. I am telling you about my good laying hens!"

"Yawari love eggs, especially when they got young, "Sylvie confirmed.

"You miss any chickens?"

"I don't think so, but they will be disappearing next."

"My white hen hatch the loveliest bunch last week," Evelyn offered, gathering up her dress and tucking the end into her waistband. She was ready to start. She paced about nervously in the old boots, her braided hair jutting out aggressively like horns.

"Wait a minute, "cautioned Dora, "We've got to be ready for it. You can't be frightened. You can't run."

Three women with brooms, one machete, a couple of sticks, and a single obsession -- to exterminate the animal, and whatever else there was with it. The plan was to shut the gate to the bottom house, close off all the coops, make a fire in the garbage bin and smoke it out of there.

The children accustomed to playing outside, were instructed to stay in the house, and at a signal, to stomp and bang on the floor above the beam where Phil reported seeing the creature. This would force the yawari out onto the ground, into the women's trap. The smoking out was the cane field technique.

Sylvie was from Berbice and knew all about it. Before cutting the canes, they torched the fields, in what the overseers called 'controlled oil drum fires.' This was not simply to thin out the excess foliage but to get rid of the rodents and snakes that lurked there. Sylvie could tell you cane field stories to make your hair sizzle, but everyone knew of burning cane, the tendrils of soot floated over the yard whenever they burned on the coast.

The women dampened the kerchiefs that would cover their faces in the two buckets of water they had filled at the vat and brought over to the gate. Once the fire was set and the smoking drum in place, they would have to move quickly, a phalanx against the enemy.

Dora's stick had a dangerous looking curved wire at the top of it. It was the stick for picking breadfruit or star apples from the trees that grew close to the house; if you stood at the kitchen window and leaned out, you could simply hook down whatever fruit you needed.

Now she placed herself across from the china trunks, and poked and prodded the overhead beams with her stick. The children loud with accompanying shouts began their part, and suddenly a sharp rustle and a flash of tail darts across the ground.

A broom just about smothers it; it trips over a stick, behind which a boot is waiting. The animal buffeted waits, tense, tail stiff and prone, eyes beady and dangerous. An instant of confusion among the hunters, they almost give way to panic, but a second broom then a machete blow stuns it. Brownish gray with a tail that twitches now, it is caught.

Smoke from the drum rages and billows. Perhaps it will catch on to something, and start a real fire to destroy them all. Evelyn is beginning to get anxious, she shouts:

"We got him. We got him. Let's put the fire out."

"Not so fast, not yet...we know 'bout playing possum," Sylvie cries, and comes down again on the quiet figure with a broom handle.

"Hit it again," they chorus, and there is no doubt this time.

It was with a spade they picked it up. The children came to see and remember the teeth bared and sharp and still grinning, the tail stiff like pegged cord. Dora strode ahead with the heavy boots, the lifeless clump of fur on the spade held out at arm's length , far away from her body, the others following in triumph still panting from the excitement. They would dump the carcass in the alley in the back of the yard.

Then they put out the fire in the drum with buckets of water and had the children bring rags for the cleanup.

They were still talking about how they outsmarted the creature, how they cut off its exit by making a solid front with their weapons. How careful they were to keep the smoke from their faces, Sylvie's clever idea about the wet kerchiefs about their necks, then pulled over their faces at the crucial time so they looked like bandits in the movies. There was only pale smoke now as the excitement petered out in the dank murky air.

Sylvie had continued banging the beams of the bottom house. There was something about doing a job, thoroughly and well, plus she was the one with the experience in vermin, she had lived on the sugar estates.

"Come, look, there's more! She got two baby possums."

These were small, confused, vulnerable bundles of fur.

They came rushing again, the adrenaline rising, but looked disappointed, subdued now, and sorry to find out they had been right, that the animal had been feeding her young. They spaded up the crumpled bundles among the dirty damp rags on the ground.

Their own children, ragged and yelling, and excited by their stomping role in the hunt, rushed to see the rest of the kill. But the glee had disappeared, their mothers now in saddened complicity made a silent procession to the alley.

GOD

They said I had walked out on God and, long afterwards, people would look at me in a strange way. What I recalled was much simpler and hardly such a sacrilege. It was one moment, a single instant, when I refused the next step. A halt in the progression... walk off the stage, never to return.

With the fear of unknown spirits, obeah and the water people forever hovering, the church was our shield, and we did not confine ourselves to a single mode of worship.

In our yard of seven families, there were at least half a dozen religious affiliations – from Seventh Day Adventists all the way to Roman Catholic. Many nights I escaped homework to follow the drums and bugle of the Salvation Army holding meetings under the street lamp.

Until the time I was twelve and confirmed as an Anglican, I had been to church among the Brethren, the Methodists, and the Nazarenes.

I walked out of the Church of the Nazarene.

I stared Sister Russell in the eye, dropped the placard that I was supposed to carry in the Jesus pageant, climbed down from the stage and strode out of the door.

Sister Russell was so dumbfounded, that she stood like a huge monument in the doorway, for a long time watching until I turned the corner into Laluni Street. It embarrassed my folks; my mother wondered for many weeks if she would be welcome at Friday night meetings, or if they would censure her for raising an unruly child.

I had reacted to Sister Russell calling me a fool. I knew I was not, but she seemed so righteous and sure that it had seemed pointless to argue. I stood with my placard, and in her exasperation at the half dozen children who could not remember whether we had planned to stand from left-to - right or right-to-left to spell out M-I-R-A-C-L-E-S, she grabbed me and vented her annoyance.

Everyone heard her call me a fool, and the other children laughed. I had no recourse, but to leave. I recall from such a long time back, the sense of having arrived at a limit. I was not angry. The situation had reached its dead end. No turns - - action was inevitable in only one direction.

I think that the clarity of the simple decision that I made resolved for me a series of strains that I had been having with Nazarene from the time we had started attending it the previous year. We had come from a little bottom-house Sunday school, a low-keyed gathering on Sunday afternoons, whose purpose was to make sure that children of folks who called themselves Christians learned something about the faith, through verses and Bible stories.

Two little, old ladies, Miss Mentore and Miss Butcher, who ran it, taught basic golden rule: do onto others, honor thy father and thy mother, and stories about the life of Moses and Jesus. It was the Brethren sect, but they did not evangelize strongly among the children, they merely wanted to gather us in. Sometimes we had lantern lectures, shadowy blinking postcards of places abroad, geography via missionary work slides, or Bible stories illustrated. It was low-keyed and comforting,, not heavy on sin and punishments, and we looked forward to dressing up in our Sunday best for these outings.

Then came the big American church, Nazarene, its bright new stone and glass building; brand new organ; and with all that came class distinctions, being saved, and bringing souls and dollars to Jesus. I was never comfortable there.

My teachers looked at me as if I were stubborn, because though visibly moved on many occasions, I never once approached the altar to be saved. Even when the choir singing tugged at my emotions, and the evangelist was a fraction away from tears, I held out.

"Don't let Satan have his way, don't let him hold you back from salvation," the minister would urge. All of my little classmates went up, crying out how badly they had sinned, how they tossed in an ocean of sin until Jesus redeemed them. I watched skeptically from my seat and held my ground. I knew even then that Sister Russell had marked me.

My departure was inevitable; the placard incident was the push I needed.

DADA

If I start at the beginning, I need to tell about Dada late at night in the half dark light on her stoop. We would try to delay going home to sleep so she would tell us stories we had heard before and surely didn't believe.

"This is how the village I was born came to be called Beterverwagting."

"How, Dada?" we would ask, pretending interest. We knew from school that the villages on the banks of the Demerara were named by the owners of sugar estates, the Dutch, the English, the French. Beterverwagting was Dutch as were Vreed-en-hoop, Uitvlugt, and Der Kinderen.

She would fold me into her lap, holding me with her crippled left arm, which was as thin and frail as my own seven-year-old child's arm only longer. Then her eyes would flash and she would gesticulate with her good arm as she told the story of the man on the bus who when he heard the price of the bus fare from the Public Road into that village, said to the driver with great indignation:

"What! All of that money just to drive in? No way, better for walk in!" (that's "better for walk in" for Beterverwagting, in case you missed it).

We laughed as we were expected to do, then she told of the same man who went to the market where a vendor had a tray of fruit.

"How much for that fruit? It looks delicious."

"Two bits," the vendor replied.

The man put his arm akimbo and exclaimed:

"What! So expensive for that fruit. Man go!"

So it was that the fruit came to be called mango. As we sat in the moonlight with a basket of long mangoes, spice mangoes, cayenne mangoes, the yellow juice dripping down our faces, this was indeed paradise.

Our mother's voice calling us in to bed because tomorrow was a school day, was a sad interruption, and Dada turned in to her own solitary bed.

Before she was our grandmother, our Dada, they called her Nina, a contortion of her given name, Claradina. Her closest friend and protector for most of her life was her first cousin Lily, who was just one year older.

When Nina was seven, she contracted polio and her parents took her to see a doctor who advertised a new electrical treatment. Nina had to place her hand on the machine, and the nurse applied pressure. She did not cry out when they increased the charge, she was speechless, in shock, her face contorted in pain. Only when her tears fell, did the nurse realize that Nina's muscles and nerves had been damaged.

The arm grew long, but did not develop in size or strength. Nina's personality suffered too; she became self-conscious and apologetic, never esteeming herself as attractive or capable.

She faded into menial jobs in other people's households and even her pregnancy came as a surprise to her. Lily stood by her without a word of disapproval or blame.

Nina wore long sleeved dresses to hide her withered arm as much as to conform to the tenets of her religion as a member of Pilgrim Holiness. The dowdy dresses that reached her ankles had not saved her from men's attentions.

Her church deemed all pleasure a sin. They had prayer meetings every night, and held strict prohibitions against dancing, wearing make-up, going to the cinema. Lily was there to help again when eight years later Nina had her second daughter.

Lily became the child's godmother, her Nen, and they baptized her in the Catholic Church, and named her Dora, which means gift from God. Indeed, Dora grew and prospered.

After years of hard work and precarious lodgings, Nina came to live within easy reach of her daughter Dora and grandchildren--at long last, in a place of her own.

It was a small apartment, two rooms and a kitchen with bath and toilet just outside the kitchen door shared with the tenant of the adjoining apartment. It was heaven to Dada, who had spent most of her life "stopping" at other people.

Dada covered every bit of wall space with family photographs and an array of garish religious pictures framed in passé partout that she had collected and grown attached to over the years. She saved newspaper clippings about the successes of her grandchildren and found every opportunity to share them with her visitors.

When Dada lived at Lot 10 the yard had mellowed, the squabbling children had grown up and moved away and the aunts rented mostly to mature working people.

AUNT CIL

We remembered the sisters by their labels: Irene, the oldest was selfish, wanting the best for herself and defrauding everyone else to achieve it, Eugenie the one who had died,

Priscilla, our Aunt Cil, the saint who sacrificed herself to help others; and Margaret, the youngest, motherless and wild, the one who became our grandmother.

They were Sir Carrie's daughters. He left Barbados in 1880 and carved out his homestead in BG. He sent his two sons back to be educated at Codrington College and they both ended up in America and earned his extreme bitterness. He went on to produce three other sons that stayed in BG, before he brought himself a new bride from his homeland.

My grandmother produced my father, my Uncle Fred and a bevy of aunts, and as she matured, she became skilled at herbs and remedies. People would come to her for balms and pain-killers, and bring their babies to have their ears pierced.

Aunt Cil remained unmarried and alone. "Poor me one," she would say, "I don't have a chick nor a child," yet she was hardly ever seen without children hanging from her arms.

We sat among her faded photographs and relived the drama of their lives. With the Brothers Grimm as our guide, we had the power to create the most lurid melodramas from anything we heard. Our family history had its share of cruel stepmothers, children starved and beaten, wicked wiles to keep lovers apart, and poisonings and suicides with household fluids.

Aunt Cil was the keeper of the flame, the one who wrote letters and told the stories. Besides Readers Digest that arrived monthly from America, Aunt Cil's favorite books were Victorian novels where the heroine, subject to trials and tribulations, always triumphed in the end. We listened open-mouthed to the story of Beauty Darling, once adored but now cast out, accused of stealing a ring that a careless magpie had taken away in its beak. We understood the cruelty of Fate, for Aunt Cil's life was itself a testimony.

Years earlier when she was young, around the time of World War I, Aunt Cil's only beau had left for America and promised to send for her. Her sister Irene, intent on keeping her home as her baby-sitter, was the one who had foiled the romance. She intercepted the boyfriend's letters, and Aunt Cil believed that he had abandoned her. The truth came out too late and Aunt Cil resigned herself to a life of hardship where she had to cut and contrive to survive and maintain her respectability. She often announced her independence from men:

"No man can hang his hat in my house, and no man can say to me, black is my eye."

By the time we lived there, Aunt Cil and my grandmother managed the family property. Aunt Cil was the serious landlord, the keeper of records and receipt books. Every month she made the pilgrimage downtown to pay taxes and fire insurance, and sometimes on school holidays, I accompanied her.

The center of Georgetown was an awe-inspiring place with its stately buildings and broad avenues flanked by flamboyant trees. I remember the dark mahogany interior of the ornate Victorian building that was our Town Hall, and the clerks with their dusty ledgers under the whirring ceiling fans. When I later read Bleak House, I clearly understood the scene that Dickens described.

After leaving the Hand-in-Hand insurance building, we would walk down Water Street to Jaikaran's, her favorite shop, and buy sweets and fancy tea biscuits imported from England.

With her parasol to shade us from the sun, Aunt Cil held my hand and pointed out the special buildings as we walked home. St Georges Cathedral, where her brother Philip had preached his inaugural sermon as an Anglican priest and made the family proud, the Carnegie Library which I could join when I became seven, and Bishops, the best girls' school in the country. I looked longingly through the railings at the girls in their white games tunics playing tennis on the green lawns, and the image stayed with me.

I must go back to 1958 explain how the family home was turned into a rooming house.

This was the year of the family reunion when Brother Willie and Sister Irene were coming to visit from America. Willie had wrestled the property from the clutches of their stepmother when Sir Carrie died, and provided his sisters with a roof over their heads. There was not a night that Aunt Cil did not extol him in her prayers; and she had long forgiven her sister Irene for robbing her of a life in America.

Aunt Cil was eager to entertain her siblings, to let them see that God was still good to her, but she had little money and did not want to borrow.

Instead, she sold off one of the cottages and used the money to remodel – carve out an extra bedroom, outfit it with new furniture, new beds. This way all four of Sir Carrie's children would be together, under the same roof, in the family home, just as they were as children fifty years ago.

She expected her brother to be proud of how she had managed things, and to be happy with the food and treats she had arranged for him.

His response was exactly opposite. He shouted at her in Biblical rage:

"Fool, fool… you have sold your birthright for a mess of pottage! Why did you squander something of such value?"

Somehow, they all survived the reunion, and the visitors returned to America. Brother Willie continued to send a hundred dollars every Christmas, which Aunt Cil scrupulously shared among the relatives.

In the end, her folly proved a blessing, because with the extra bedroom upstairs, she had rooms to rent and could maintain a shelter over their heads.

DAY IS DONE

My father came home from work drenched in sweat. He rode his bicycle home as the sun fell off in intensity at four o'clock. Stripped of these clothes, he took a long cold shower, ate a bowl of porridge then, dressed in a loose cotton shirt and trousers, he sat in his Morris chair and read the newspaper then the Webster's dictionary.

He would make lists of words and study their pronunciation and meaning. Then selecting certain words that appealed to him, he would wait to challenge us when we came home from school. We were probably the only children anywhere who knew the occupation of a funambulist or a numismatist.

Every morning from seven to four in the afternoon, my father was a carpenter, with a break for his heavy meal at noon. Three or four times a week, from eight to four, he was a night watchman at Sprostons wharf on the river. He liked when people said he was a good provider; it did not occur to him that he was overworking into an early grave.

He had to fall off a roof to come to his senses.

Only then, it became clear that tradition or no, he had to look for something better.

My father had grown into the carpentry trade. He was born to a family with wood in its blood. His grandfather had built all of the houses on the property he owned. The old man could wave his hand over any street in Albertown and point out a house he had built.

These days, not much new building was going on and carpentry was hard work, even if you yourself were a contractor and got to send other men out to work in the hot sun. Those old houses built so strong, just plain lasted too long. A little repair here and there and a dash of paint, and they were as good as new.

He felt strange and numb, no pain really. He could only guess how they broke the news to his wife and six children when they rushed him to hospital. Perhaps all his bones were broken, no blood, but he was unconscious, he was sure of that. They seem to forget how lazy those hospital porters were. Unless they see blood, those fellows take their time; when they finally bring a stretcher, and check that he is not dead, they would toss him like a bag of coal, since he cannot shout out either in pain or annoyance. Then they would prop him up some place out of the way in the emergency area until someone could come to look at him.

The nurses, sulking and slow in their ill-fitting uniforms, would then come and take his pulse as if they were doing him the greatest favor. Lord only help him if he could survive hospitalization!

I was the first one reached because my school was nearest the hospital. My mother wanted me to go home and manage things while she stayed there and tried to find out how badly my father was injured.

The man who came to my school with the news was just a man my mother had met at the hospital. When he came in, he went straight into the headmaster's room, and Mr. Henry came over to my seat and touched me on the shoulder. He was so quiet and sympathetic that I wondered if the bad news meant that somebody was dead. My head was swimming when I returned with him to his room, then he told me:

"Your father was in an accident. Your mother wants you to go home". When I looked horrified, he continued, "No... nobody dead! Just go home quickly and look after the little ones."

I got home and found the neighbors all outside hoping to hear more from whoever was entering the yard.

This marked the beginning of my father's career at Bookers Security. He stayed there thirty years, eventually rising to the position of Chief.

TEACHER BOURNE

I started school at Teacher Bourne in the September after my third birthday. My baby sister Cookie was born that month and my mother had her hands full with my two-year-old brother just started to walk and getting into all sorts of trouble.

It would be an ease for my mother, everyone thought, because I was such a busy body always in her shadow, always asking questions. It was convenient too, because my sister Pam who was six and in first standard at the Catholic primary school could drop me off on her way to school.

I already knew my alphabet and I could count, so Teacher Bourne had every reason to welcome me. I can recall few details of my first days there, but I made friends and felt excited about going there, and I brought home very good reports.

Vivid memories start about age five for me, when I had established my place in the little school. We were the three Junes-- June Edwards and June Betancourt and I-- we seemed to be a preordained threesome, birthdays in the same month, playing together at recess, sharing the same storybooks, and always talking, talking... so that Teacher Bourne or Teacher Amy who took charge of singing and arithmetic for the older children, would have to say:

"June, June, June... cease your talking at once!"

June Betancourt was Portuguese and a Catholic so she was assured a place at Queenstown RC, the same primary school my sister Pam attended. Her parents let her stay an extra year with us because she was making such good progress and enjoying her time. They were the rich folk, owners of a dry goods store at First and Albert Streets.

On my way home from school in the afternoons, I would stop and play on the shop bridge that spanned the culvert separating the shop from the road. June would bring candy from her shop to share. It did not matter how dreary recitation of multiplication tables became, we knew we had play and fun to look forward to after school.

The Edwards girls were an East Indian family newly arrived from Berbice who had bought a house on our street. June and her sister Bridget attended Teacher Bourne because their house was just two doors away. I remember great resentment when Bridget got a higher score than I did on a spelling test. They did not stay long, perhaps just two terms, until they made the correct church connection for primary school.

The primary schools, overseen by the government bureau, were controlled by various church administrations. There were Catholic schools, Anglican schools, Methodists and Moravian schools. A headmaster or headmistress had to be solid in their church in order to win approval for their position, and children, admitted from age five to primary schools, had to show evidence of baptism in the appropriate religion.

The most organized schools with the best teachers and strongest scholarship record were, at this time, Catholic and Anglican schools. There were hierarchies within them but parents tried to choose schools in their own neighborhoods.

My sister Pam had been baptized in the Roman Catholic Church because my mother's best friend, chosen as godmother, was a Catholic.

My mother married at Clarkson Brethren Church and later sent us to Brethren Sunday School, but that sect was not relevant in primary schools. Christened Methodist because of my godmother, I was in jeopardy. The nearest Methodist school was all the way in Bourda, lower down the academic scale than the nearby Anglican school. We relied on Aunt Cil's connection to the Anglican Church to get me into St. Ambrose where Miss Friday was headmistress.

My friends had left and I found myself still at Teacher Bourne into my sixth birthday. In spite of small classes and much individual attention, I was bored and resentful and daydreamed about going to big school.

"When I go to big school, I am going to do longer and longer sums, and I will have many, many books with lots and lots of pictures."

I recall drowsy afternoons, the sun so hot and not a shiver of breeze as we rocked together singing our times tables. I would look at the clock and try to measure how long it took to get to two o'clock, when the school day ended, as the long hand moved ever so slowly. Just think, in a few more such moves, time would bring me to big school.

There were some horrible times. I twice fell into the culvert and arrived home covered in mud and slime. One was a genuine accident when I was looking into the water at the fish and slipped. The other time, I felt sure that Daphne had pushed Lambert and me into the ditch when we were all sheltering from the rain under the eaves of Betancourt's shop. Daphne who was bigger had begun to set the other children against me by calling me a show off and telling lies about me. One of her lies was that Lambert was my boyfriend. I met her on the playground, hit her, and we ended up tussling on the ground.

Teacher Bourne did not approve of hooliganism and kept us both after school. She made us sweep the floors and stack the benches, and then she lectured us about decent behavior and had us read and copy a verse from Proverbs. It was around this time that Teacher Bourne devised other ways to ease what she felt was my boredom.

She made me a sort of assistant teacher and in the quiet after school, she would tutor me in advanced grammar and arithmetic herself. In that way, she explained I would be ready for anything they came with at big school. I wanted to be brilliant when I got there so that she would be proud of me.

I became enthusiastic about school again and waited for late afternoon when the sun had become more forgiving, and the noise of chanting and recitation had ceased. She introduced me to books far more interesting than Nelson West Indian Readers and Kate and Lay grammar books; these always had short bits of stories and I used to wonder what became of the rest of the book. I now read Aesop's fables and Just So Stories.

I saw the envy in Daphne's eyes and felt good about my new status.

HUGO

I have been a teacher from the age of seven. Teacher Bourne set me the task of teaching Hugo to write.

Do not write for him! Guide Hugo's hand so that he writes a slate full of strokes.

She had patiently raised me with much the same technique, from the intellectual stage of nothing, which Hugo now occupied, to a precocious literacy and expert knowledge of analysis and parsing.

"Yes, Teacher Bourne." I answered dutifully.

As she waddled away from me in her schoolteacher's blue tunic and white lace blouse, I placed my hand over Hugo's. He was not paying attention; he wanted to look around at everything else in the room, his brain totally disconnected from the arm that I was pointlessly dragging across the slate. And Hugo drooled.

Hugo was five and just as tall as I was. His hand trembled when I increased the pressure of my fingers so the pencil could make short vertical lines in neat rows on the ruled lines of his slate. His tongue stayed at half-mast between his open lips, and bubbles of saliva formed at the corner of his mouth. Whenever I would give his arm a hard yank, to start another line of strokes, a trickle of spit would fall off the edge of his chin, land in a large slimy droplet on his hand then trail away onto mine.

I looked up in alarm for Teacher Bourne but she was busy with arithmetic class, waving her ruler like a conductor as the children sang the multiplication tables.

"Three times ten are thirty, thirty, thirty, three times ten are thirty, and one makes thirty-one, thirty-two…"   *LOL*

It had just rained -- a short sudden blast that rattled accompaniment on the tin roofs and gutters of her house. In the safe shelter of her bottom house school, we watched the rain stir up the dust in the little patch of playground outside, and raise a curtain of steamy haze that tickled our noses. The rain made the leaves glisten and the bright red hibiscus flowers on her garden hedge looked brighter and redder as the sun came out again.

Hugo was my designated problem for that morning. I had a little brother at home, so I knew boys and thought myself to be kind -hearted. I stopped our writing and rummaged in Hugo's clothes for his handkerchief. I found his folded cotton square tucked into the elastic band of his khaki shorts. Mothers dressed children carefully in those days; anyway, this was before the invention of Kleenex.

I looked at our handiwork. Many of the strokes were wiggly, but reasonably vertical. I used the trail of Hugo's spit and the sweat on my fingertips to erase the unredeemable crooked lines, then, I decided that Hugo should write by himself, without my guiding hand. My fingers were stiff and I was quite uncomfortable, squeezed so closely to Hugo on the tiny wooden bench. I stood up and decided to oversee his efforts.

interesting

The first thing Hugo did was to change the slate pencil from his right hand to his left. Then he arched his body over his slate and in a concentrated torrent of drool, filled the space on the slate with the neatest, straightest vertical strokes that anyone, even Teacher Bourne, could ever want.

Of course, if she had spotted his ruse, Teacher Bourne would have rapped his knuckles sharply with her wooden ruler; she was convinced that left-handedness was a correctable condition and had put considerable effort into curing Hugo of this shame.

On the other hand, I was a complete pragmatist, concerned strictly with the product. I would not have cared if Hugo produced a slate of straight strokes with his toes. From here, he would graduate to curves, then circles, then all the letters of the alphabet. I wanted Hugo to be happy that he had produced something good, and to feel confident that he could learn more and look forward to what came next.

Soon he would be writing letters to his parents and getting to know pen pals in other countries! I praised his success and promised him a marble if he would do a perfect slate of strokes again.

It was lunchtime and I had to help with the smaller children, peel their bananas for them and see that they did not spill their drinks. I left Hugo in a corner, contorted over his slate, far from Teacher Bourne's eyes.

In the close, stale air of the bottom house school, a child's day was a tedium of reading, writing, recitation and dusty recess -- but I remember my guilty thrill as I tried to communicate to Hugo that he was on the verge of an exciting new world.

ST. AMBROSE

On the day that Aunt Cil took me to register at St. Ambrose, we again heard that the school was too full and that first standard, where most seven year olds would fit, had an influx of graduates from preparatory classes everywhere.

Aunt Cil knew the headmistress Miss Friday; she was a fellow office holder in the Anglican Churchwomen's guild.

So, whereas other parents and their children were turned away, we were given chairs and told to wait. I sat on the edge of the scholarship class that was set up outside the headmistress' office. These were a dozen or so ten and eleven year old trainees for the best high schools, and they were aware of their special status as the elite of the primary school.

As I waited, I copied from the blackboard some of their assignments and proceeded to do them. By the time Miss Friday called me in, I had a slate full of long divisions, and I was in the process of making sentences with the vocabulary words. I started to put away my slate so that I could greet her politely, but she took hold of it, turned it over and asked:

"What work is this?"

"Just what they are doing outside", I replied, hoping that I had not transgressed and lost my chance.

Did you do these? She asked me again and when I said yes, she began to question me about grammar and arithmetic and I answered just as Teacher Bourne had taught me.

I thought you told me she was coming from nursery school? How can I put her in first standard?

Miss Friday looked disgruntled.

Aunt Cil could only say that I loved schoolwork and was bright and she hoped Miss Friday had some place in her school to put me.

I was placed in third standard with classmates who were mostly nine and ten, and the teacher made me sit up front close to her desk so she could see me.

Third standard was in the upper school building, a huge main hall with dividers separating classrooms that held twenty or thirty students. In the mornings, the dividers between classes swung aside and we rose and faced the stage, an elevated platform at the end. The entire east side had glass windows facing out onto the street and honors boards occupied its other three sides. These oblongs of highly polished mahogany bore the names of scholarship winners in gold Gothic script.

Names and dates went far back into the century, and it was a thrill to recognize that important people, like our Minister of Education, had been a student in this same primary school, and a scholarship win had opened the way for him.

We sang hymns, said prayers from the Book of Common Prayer, heard the day's announcements and recited the school pledge:

"I pledge myself to uphold the good name of St. Ambrose School.

I will be true and just in all my conduct.

I will learn to serve my country loyally.

I will do my duty to God, the Queen, and all men.

So help me God."

My classmates sat in rows of benches, a long desk beside each row, and in front, a blackboard balanced precariously on an easel.

I had never been in a class with so many people and I felt very small at the edge of the bench nearest the teacher. All of the other students knew each other because they had come through the previous classes, and their ways were different from anything I knew.

You did not use a slate in middle school so I got my first set of exercise books, and a common pen and a set of nibs. A fountain pen was something very special; our teacher had two, one with blue ink and the other red that she used to correct our work. Exercise books had a pale blue cover with a picture of the ruling monarch on the front and a list of useful tables of weights and measures on the back.

Our wooden desks had holes for inkwells and a shelf below to hold our books. When six students occupied a single desk meant for four, not only were they scrunched together on the bench, their elbows touched when they tried to write and ink frequently spilled.

There were blackboard monitors and ink monitors. Blackboard monitors made sure the erasers were clean, and would be responsible for adjusting and moving the board for the teacher's convenience. Ink monitors had to mix ink in jars from ink powder and water, and make sure the inkwells on each desk were full before the class writing exercise began.

Our teacher was Miss Horsham. She was very protective of me and seemed very pleased that I understood whatever she explained with little difficulty.

From the other students in class I could sense a world of gossip and jokes I did not understand, so I bided my time and did not rush to raise my hand too often but would sit quietly pretending to be humble.

Only when the teacher's mounting frustration at the incomprehension of the class threatened to be bad for everyone, would I offer a solution and save the day. This style won me some friends among these older children who could

Survival skills

just have easily despised me; I never flaunted and often
helped people with their homework, so I felt protected by
them even though I wasn't much happier when they replaced
Shorty, their first nickname for me, with Genius.

As soon as I had proved myself in that class and adjusted to
life in primary school, Miss Friday began to groom me as a
scholarship prospect.

My transition to primary school was not without its
heartaches. I tempered my eagerness to do perfect school
exercises and win teachers approval with a modest
offhandedness that endeared me to some classmates. Others,
like Leonie and the Macalman sisters resisted, and found ways
to tease and torment me. They told secrets behind their
hands, laughed and conspired against me.

We wore uniforms of brown tunics and cream blouses, and
hats for the hot sun at noon. A monitor collected our hats for
the hat room, then handed them out after class.

My hat was conspicuous; not a simple straw hat but one
handed down from my aunt, and though cream with a brown
band, it was obviously not a child's hat.

Leonie and her gang would pass the hat from one to another
shrieking with laughter while I shrank in embarrassment.

Only with time did I learn repartee and toughness, and could
counter any insult with one of my own. "I thief your mother
white fowl?" I could rejoin if anyone stared at me.

Another terror of primary school life was corporal punishment. Each teacher possessed a bamboo cane and the prerogative to use it on pupils.

Punishment in a group was annoying but not serious; a teacher would spray the shoulders of a giggly group if she thought they were inattentive, or swish their legs with the cane if they were standing in line and talking, but these were not emotional issues even though some students cried.

The trouble came when individual students were made to stand out of class then whipped in front of everyone else. I prayed that this would never happen to me as I watched frequent offenders face the cane. Our teacher would sometimes relent and send students un-whipped back to their places. Perhaps she felt that the mere threat of punishment was enough.

When I think of Simon Legree, I see the face of Mr. Sobers, one of the two male teachers in the school. Unlike Mr. Mac who joked with students, Mr. Sobers smiled only when he saw a parade of latecomers taking their place outside the headmistress' door.

"Let me handle this matter", he would say, and Miss Friday would demur.

sadistic

Briskly, and with obvious delight, Mr. Sobers, deaf to all excuses, would dispense a pair of sharp whip cracks in the palm of each student before sending them off to their classes.

He wore his cane as part of his uniform and offered his services to any teacher who had students standing out in front of their classes. It was no use arguing; Mr. Sobers' philosophy was that punishment should be short, swift and severe.

He had perfected his instrument; lithe and supple it was, he could bend it in a perfect arc when he held its handle in one hand and its tip in the other, and when he raised it in the air it would sing in a high whine before it landed on the palm of its cringing victim.

Some pupils claimed they used jumbie bubbie, a certain fruit whose pulp if rubbed on the hand toughened the palm and took the sting out of the lash, but others claimed that the same fruit made the red welts on their hands burst into sores. All grimaced, and some cried, but many frequent offenders were known to fake their shouts and earned themselves bonus lashes.

The severest punishment was six lashes on the seat of the pants: a boys' punishment, this was a terrifying experience for the victim as well as the watchers. Aware of Mr. Sobers' skill, few boys could treat this lightly so they devised many schemes. Wearing double trousers or having thick khaki shorts soaked in salt made a loud sound but reduced the damage.

In the afternoons, at the end of the school day, we filed out for afternoon play, the short respite before scholarship lessons.

We would rush outdoors and select our teams for rounders or dog and the bone. The games we liked best were the ones that were energetic and made us laugh and shout and run, all of the pleasures denied during our day of classroom drudgery in the conspicuous scholarship class outside Miss Friday's office.

We were on our best behavior as representatives of the school if visitors came; but all day we had arduous exercises in arithmetic, grammar and composition. The exam was a constant motivation and a constant threat; this was our big chance. There was nothing abstract about it, it was real to us all: a scholarship win led to the country's best school and a future in a profession: teacher, lawyer, or doctor.

We needed a raucous outlet to balance the constrained mental activity of our training; everyone knew that too much study could make one mad. We had examples all around us, and though we children mocked the humorous antics of local eccentrics, our parents and teachers treated them with sympathy.

Profit Wills would appear at our classroom from time to time, and though the students giggled to see him in tattered top hat reciting Shakespeare, the teachers invited him into the staff room and treated him well.

Bertie Van was once a respected schoolmaster who now roamed the streets with all his worldly goods tied in a bundle on his bike, and Bob Adams and British Walker were bright, educated men who now wandered in the streets bathed in sweat, talking to their demons.

So we played for all our worth, running and cavorting and having snacks of lemonade and buns until it was time for our special after-school lessons to begin. We looked forward to the afternoon lessons, we were happy to stay long and late competing among ourselves and sharpening our intellectual senses.

The school was now quiet, regular students all gone home, leaving just the sweepers, a dozen scholarship hopefuls and Miss Friday.

MISS FRIDAY

Our school centennial song was set to a calypso beat, and we swung our hips and belted out its name in the chorus: St. Ambrose, St. Ambrose!

Miss Friday was retiring after decades of service, and staid propriety gave way to months of celebration.

St. Ambrose was founded in 1855 just twenty-one years after the abolition of slavery in the colonies. Miss Friday, trained in England, was the first local woman to become its headmistress, and now at 55, she had reached mandatory retirement age.

In a series of variety concerts, students showed their talent in music, song and dance. Famous alumni returned to visit, recalling the glory days of the school, and dignitaries showered Miss Friday with awards. I was now in my third year and caught up in all the exciting events.

The only sad corollary in our school's special year was that we had no scholarship winners. Miss Friday's two brightest pupils each scored 65%, a score termed "qualified" for limited benefits in certain secondary schools.

We said good-bye to Miss Friday whom we loved despite her seriousness, and looked with apprehension to the new headmaster, Mr. Henry, coming from the wilds of Belladrum, in Berbice.

QUEEN AND COUNTRY

Ten thousand feet in puttees, a thousand black faces in white dresses waving small flags, red, white and blue; throngs of schoolchildren in tunics of every color, marching from the hot asphalt streets into the green oasis of Durban Park racetrack.

Children of the Empire
Come raise your voices
Hail we with joy our Queen today
One with the Empire in love and in loyalty
Gladly our homage now we pay

.....

We sing with heart and soul this chorus
God bless the Empire, God Save the Queen

True, the Queen was far away in England, and we were schoolchildren in a tiny country on the edge of South America. British Guiana was the only British colony in that continent, the single blob of colonial pink on the map in our atlas; we were the only English speakers, the last bastion of the Union Jack.

In 1953, the first two hours of most school mornings we spent in marching drill as we prepared for the Coronation of Queen Elizabeth II on June 2.

Besides our headmistress, Mr. Hamlet our marching instructor was the most important person in our school for the six months before the Coronation.

Dressed in our brown tunics and cream-colored blouses, we would line up in threes on the pavement in front of our school promptly at 8am. Mr. Hamlet would first drill us individually, his intention to ensure that we were alert and awake.

"Left turn, right turn!"

"By the left, quick march!"

"Halt!

Halt, means stop at once!

Child, which is your left hand? Show me.

Your left foot is just below that hand.

Close ranks. About turn. Quick march!"

The sun would start to burn and before long, the rubber soles of our yachtings -- canvas-topped shoes would be melting into the asphalt, but Mr. Hamlet wanted perfection. Most schoolchildren wore these yachtings, not because we went boating, but because they were cheap Bata shoes made in India. Leather English shoes that cost a week's wages, were worn sparingly and kept for Sundays.

Once he had inspected the ranks, he made us mark time, lifting our heels in place until we had developed unison of rhythm and stride, then we set out to march down Third Street through Cummings Street and back along North Road. We would stop at the major roads to let traffic go by, but otherwise the carts and bicycles, and pedestrians, stood at the parapet and shouted encouragement and admiration to us as we marched swinging our arms and keeping step to our commander's call.

Mr. Hamlet had been a drill sergeant in the Army in World War II, and though he had not been called overseas to defend the Mother Country he took his allegiance to the Queen seriously, and refused to be swayed by exhausted, silly schoolchildren longing to get back to shade and relief of the school building.

The big event would take place in Durban Park, the horse race course and cricket club. We would march from thence to the Parade Ground for the trooping of the colors ceremony and presentation of arms, with the governor in regalia and plumed hat with his entourage.

Ladies wore hats and gloves and had white parasols to protect them from the sun. Government ministers and their wives -- the local versions of the English gentry-- sat on the podium. All the parents and other people filled up the seats and bleachers while the loud speakers and cricket scoreboards announced their single message: "God Save the Queen!"

After the Coronation, we enjoyed the souvenirs, new Royal pictures on the walls of our homes and school. Then life went back to normal, waiting for scholarship results, or the anxiety of getting a job if you were in sixth standard at the end of primary schooling.

It was a world of few opportunities; unless you were chosen early for an elite high school. At sixteen, you could take an exam that qualified you for teacher training, or apprentice even earlier to learn a trade. The other choice was to find any work to feed your family and live.

People were content to live the lives their parents lived until the new politics gave them hope that their lives could be very different and should be worth more; young locals who had studied abroad were returning to change their country.

Idealistic, some with trade union backgrounds, trained across the range of professions, they called themselves Marxist socialists. The formed a political party and set up cadres to educate the masses, not only about their political rights but also about the world around them and their place in it.

The Peoples Political Party (PPP), led by an East Indian dentist and a Black barrister had run in the first election in 1953 where there was universal suffrage, and they won an astounding victory.

This was the first step to Independence, they thought, but Britain, unsure of their direction, had curbed their advance. The British government revoked the constitution and some of the party's leaders were imprisoned. British warships docked in our harbor and troops came ashore to secure the colony.

In 1957 Ghana gained its Independence. We frolicked in the streets in pride for Kwame Nkrumah, and hope for our own country. Kente cloth was seen everywhere; women wore dresses with Nkrumah's face wrapped proudly around their behinds. All the talk was about freedom.

The benevolent Queen became the symbol of our bondage; we needed to shake off the shackles of colonialism.

The first casualty was the old Queen. One night, Victoria's statue was blasted with dynamite from in front of the Victoria Law Courts in Brickdam. The abstraction of freedom became a threat, and we began to live in dangerous times. *True*

EXAM

On the day after the scholarship results came out, my father woke early and with manic energy began to tear away the shingles that covered the sides of our cottage.

"I am going to throw this house up in the air," he said, "Fence in the bottom house, and dash on a couple coats of paint."

This had been his frequent mantra but we had no idea that he meant to plunge ahead all by himself so early on a Sunday morning.

He assured my mother that when people looked down First Street, they would see a decent house befitting a Bishops girl.

Our weather beaten gray shingles had always been a sore point, more especially since some Americans, visiting our neighbor, had pointed to our house and asked:

"Who lives in that broken down cabin?"

That remark had annoyed my father. He sucked his teeth in disgust when we reported it:

"What are they calling a cabin? They think this is Uncle Tom's slavery days… What do they know? This is a good, solid house!"

Except for its red door, we could not even say what color house we lived in, so mottled and worn were its shingles and so crooked its roof. Squeezed up against the palings of the neighboring yard, in the armpit of an enormous sapodilla tree, our house bore the brunt of broken branches and always had its gutters clogged with leaves.

When it rained, the gutters overflowed and broke away from their down-spouts. In season when the sapodillas ripened and their rich, heavy smell dominated dusk time fruit bats would nest in the ceiling of our house and come out to scare us at odd times during the day.

Our house was not a source of joy but we tolerated it because we owned it, and could not go elsewhere to rent because we lived among relatives on the family property.

When he knew that I had won a scholarship, and was set to enter the country's best school, my father got the impetus he needed to change our family's status.

He was always saying: "I have plans, lots of plans. Just waiting for the right time."

He said it so often that we paid no heed. He must have hardly slept because the excitement and congratulations had begun the day before when they broke the news to us, before it came out in all three of the Sunday newspapers.

The news came Saturday, a day for shopping and major chores. My mother did the marketing with my brother and my sisters and I did cleaning and laundry.

My task was to scrub the front and back stairs of our house, and my mother was particular in her warning to me because she knew I hurried through my chores so that I could escape somewhere with a book.

"I want those boards so clean that I could eat off them. No lick and promise. Scrub them till they are white!"

Just when I had emptied the scrub bucket and was hanging the cloths to dry on the banister, I looked up to see my headmaster wheeling his bicycle into our yard. I was first embarrassed because I was wearing old and tattered clothes, then excitement stirred.

Word had been going around about scholarship results, the exam that we had taken two months ago, so his visit had to mean something important.

The scholarship exam was the main event for primary schools. The cream of its crop could win a place at the best government high schools, and the headmaster's duty was to build his school's reputation and his own on the quantity of scholarships won.

Children trained for these exams from the age of eight taking lessons after school, and many families trimmed their food budget to be able to afford outside tutors to enhance their children's chances.

Mr. Robinson was a highly sought-after tutor, flying from place to place on his bicycle for business. He was always tired and sweating and the itinerant life was taking its toll.

He became much more productive when my father, in exchange for his services to me, allowed him to hold classes in our house four days a week. I had "qualified" the previous year and my parents were putting all resources behind me this time.

My mother started her preparations many weeks before the exam, feeding me callaloo and fish head soup, known brain foods. On the morning of the exam, she fed me a boiled egg with my tea. Then I set out with my mother's wrist- watch on my arm, my Cousin Andrew's Parker 51 fountain pen, and a pair of cloves in my shoes for good luck.

The Scholarship exam had very strict rules. Only the candidates and civil service adjudicators were permitted on the site. As the ten and eleven year old pupils filed in, parents and an assortment of teachers and tutors, gathered at the shop across the street and waited for the children to emerge at lunch recess. There were two hours for Arithmetic in the morning, a break, then two hours of Composition followed by an hour of General Intelligence test.

At the end of the day, Mr. Robinson flew out from under the cake shop to greet me, and after reviewing my answers, assured me that I had done well.

Now it seemed that the waiting was over, results were out.

Mr. Henry, the headmaster of my school was coming up the walk and I dashed indoors to make myself presentable.

"Oh, my God, results are out," my mother exclaimed.

Then she threw open the front door and I heard her taking the situation in hand:

"It's OK to leave your bicycle there, Mr. Henry, come right in. What a pleasure to see you!"

Mr. Henry bounded up my freshly scrubbed steps, a cryptic smile on his face in a vain attempt to contain his excitement. His wide-hipped body in an everyday plaid shirt and belted gray pants, instead of his schoolmaster tweeds and tie, made him look like ordinary folk.

As I emerged, this stranger rushed past my mother and scooped me up.

"Girl, girl", he exclaimed, "You put we on top, top of the world!"

He was stammering in Creolese, and it did not even matter to him. He hugged my mother, grandmother, everyone in sight.

Then my mother screamed for the whole yard to hear: "Results are out! She passed!"

I had barely taken this all in, when I looked up to see Mr. Robinson, my tutor, wheeling his bicycle into the yard, his sweating face in a broad grin. He connected first with my father rushing up from the backyard in response to my mother's screams.

"Your lordship," Robinson exclaimed, dropping his bike and opening his arms in a grandiloquent gesture, "what did I tell you?"

And he kept on talking, attracting a crowd in the yard, flailing his arms with all the drama that he usually saved for describing cricket matches.

"Number one! Just like I predicted! Primero! What you say to that?"

And with the sun beating down, and Robinson wiping his drenched face with his big handkerchief, and everyone talking at the same time, my father did not have the heart to tell him that Mr. Henry had preceded him, had come first with the news and taken away his thunder.

We wondered how the two men would greet each other; the legitimate headmaster flaunting his school's reputation and the interloper, this tireless itinerant outsider whose livelihood depended on individual success. To whom was the honor due? Was there enough glory to share?

My father entered the house with one arm around Mr. Robinson and placed his other arm around Mr. Henry. Everyone seemed to be talking at once at the top of their voices, and only when they sat down and each commandeered a glass could we make sense of all the news. A tray of glasses, ice, a bottle of homemade sorrel drink, some soda; my mother was quick with the refreshments and setting everyone at ease.

We need something stronger, my father said, and the celebration rum, at least ten years old, was brought out. Mr. Henry and Mr. Robinson were sorting out the details of percentages; I had scored 90% and was first -- the next in line was not even close at 85 or 86 % and went to a boy from the Catholic school.

As they clinked their glasses, to celebrate that I had not only passed, but "topped the colony", the two men beamed at everyone and at each other because there was enough happiness to dispel any bad feelings at least for a time.

As the subject of their jubilation, I stood apart, silent, no one asked my opinion about anything just then. I took in the happiness that was exploding all around me as the neighbors hearing the excitement walked in through our open door and joined in.

My mother put out more glasses and sent my brother down the road to Mr. Yhap's grocery shop for more soft drinks.

BISHOPS

Bishops marked people for life. A small girls' school of 400 pupils in a bankrupt British colony on the edge of a continent, is, in the context of the world an insignificant item.

But in the souls of the young, and the aspirations of families, Bishops was a maker of destiny. Girls were selected early; from the age of ten their future, or at any rate, the esteem in which they held themselves, was set. Valued, sorted, and graded by whatever talent, intellect or grace they were found to lack or possess, they left childhood behind them and awoke to a new perspective of the world.

In 1956, I entered Bishops as a scholarship winner. As insurance, I had also taken the entrance examination for the school, which required, beyond the academic test, a personal interview with the headmistress and her deputy.

I remember the trauma in our household over what I should wear and how exactly I should present myself. My people were humble, no claim to important family connections nor the social set that appeared in newspapers, but we were not bumpkins; we were city folk and knew a few things.

I would not wear church clothes and certainly not anything gaudy that could be mistaken for party wear. I was to be neat, business-like but fresh and youthful.

My mother despised the sad self-effacing look meant to represent the virtues of modesty and humility, but instead turned out the miserable children she deemed "old people pickney".

I wore a white pique box pleated dress that my mother had sewed for me. It was almost like a games tunic, except it had short sleeves. And I wore good English brown shoes, Clark's, with white anklets. Black ribbons at the tips of my paired braids and my mother's wristwatch completed the outfit and I felt as crisp and efficient as I looked when I walked into the room to greet Miss Harris and Miss Dewar.

Miss Harris stretched out her hand and took mine in a strong but loose-wristed handshake. Her blue eyes were kind as she asked me why I wanted to attend Bishops.

"Because it is the most recognized school in the colony," was my rehearsed reply. I looked around the room furnished exactly as I expected from the Angela Brazil girls' school novels that I devoured.

There were the mahogany bookcases, rich brown and black leather; the vase of fresh bougainvillea and rattan side chairs were the only reminders of our tropical location. I could almost relax except for the silent piercing eyes of Miss Dewar, the deputy headmistress. With her hair a severe braided coronet about her head, she seemed to distrust everything about me. She was a local success, the first female to win the Guyana scholarship for study in England. Now she was set to become the first local headmistress of Bishops as soon as the English woman's contract ended.

After questions about my hobbies, and questions about my family, all meant to put me at ease, which Miss Harris managed with the smiling condescension I expected, there was a passage I had to read aloud first, before answering questions.

It was an unfamiliar piece, unlike any from the books that I was reading at that time, and I faltered for the first time. I had to speculate on the motives of the character in the piece, to use my imagination, to express myself.

At the end, both women rose and shook my hand. It was a very adult session, a small child being received and treated as a serious person.

For me that always characterized what Bishops meant--a sense of place, person and pride. Much later, even when I understood how much damage Bishops had caused in some people's lives, I never lost the thrill of being in the main arena watching it happen.

The girls who had been in preparatory forms established their identity as the rich girls, since their parents paid fees and spared them the banality of public elementary schools. They had also been spared the vicious competitiveness of the scholarship examinations.

By third form they had organized themselves into various cliques, knew each other well and waited for the new class, which included the scholarship winners from all over the country.

Everyone looked the same; uniform requirements were stringently observed.

Cloth for our tunics could be bought only by special dispensation from Fogarty's, green casement cotton, and the tunic itself was to be made so that the hem was four inches deep and two and a half inches above the ground when the student kneeled. Cotton flannel knickers, Panama hat with a two-inch brim, green flannel blazer, and all of the accessories crests, hatbands, imported from England.

We all rode bicycles to school, no more than two abreast. The rules and standards of Bishops were made clear to us. Prefects, the senior sixth form class would always be present, on site and off, to ensure that we preserved the good name of our school.

I remember the butterflies of nervous expectation, the sheer awe of entering the hallowed halls, learning the school hymn and motto; and the relief once I had survived the first week and had some sense of what my path would be.

But everyone did not meet Bishops with the same level of self confidence. The mental separation came early, the strong from the weak, with few allowed to fall into the chasm in between.

For the first term the class leaders of 3B, my form, were old girls who knew the ropes, who were expected to show the rest of us how things were done at Bishops. How teachers were escorted to classes from the staff room and how to greet them in class; the fine points of classroom decorum -- how treats were shared, gifts bought, and friendships maintained.

There were enough of us new girls not to feel threatened but the mystique of the place made us watch with docility and copy the others.

There were so many new subjects: Geometry. Algebra, French, Latin and English Literature; I was awed by the sheer quantity of schoolbooks that I now possessed.

The greatest intellectual thrill, however, came from our formidable teachers, the academic elite who radiated confidence and demanded excellence.

By their example we learned to appreciate the subtlety of insult and the power of the withering glance; a new world opened for us and Bishops armed us with weapons to survive in it.

PLAY DATE

A high point of my first term was an invitation to visit one of our class leaders at her home. I thought at the time this was evidence of acceptance; perhaps I was merely being tested.

I rode my bicycle to Kitty to spend the afternoon with Mary. Her maid had prepared tea for us. I entered the front door of her house, and immediately I saw the table laid out with a lace tablecloth, the tray of sandwiches and cake, and place settings for two.

"Yes," Mary greeted me," that is our tea. But first we will play outdoors for a while."

I had exerted myself riding all that distance, battling the Public Road traffic of dray carts and wagons, and I would gladly have liked the relief of something cool, like lemonade as a bit of refreshment. Of course, I dare not ask.

So we went outdoors and she showed me the trees in her backyard: jamoon, that stains everything in sight an indelible purple but makes delicious wine, and a genip tree from which she reached and handily got a bunch for us to share.

"We will climb some trees, later after our games," she announced.

We jumped rope for a while, and then we were called in to tea because the maid wanted to clean up and go home. Mary's mother was a teacher and was due in from work about the time the maid planned to leave.

The tea was marvelous, I remember a very nice cake and I was able to have lemonade instead of tea as I preferred. Afterwards, Mary took me up to her room to see her books and when we were tired of that, she insisted on telling me about her ancestors and illustrious genealogy.

"Now I shall tell you about my ancestors."

I was quite startled at this as an activity. I wanted to go back outdoors to the fruit trees. But she was dead serious and she was my host.

She took out a family album and started at the beginning of a batch of spotty faded photographs of ministers and old ladies. I found the pictures fascinating, though for the most part, I ignored her spirited commentary on who they were and how they were connected to her. I sat through it all with a pleasant demeanor and thanked her for her hospitality.

I was exhausted when I rode home; it had become dusk and the traffic was lighter. I felt a sense of ease as I pedaled away convinced that I had broken through to the inner circle of BHS with my performance that afternoon.

I was learning how to get along, but I did not need to belong!

HAIR

My sin was the sin of rudeness and pride and my punishment was half-pressed hair.

I had been holding my own, answering back, buoyed by the cleverness of my banter. I never knew that I had crossed that very fine line from humor into danger.

Without another word, my mother turned off the burner of the little kerosene stove on our kitchen hearth, removed the pair of hot iron combs and wiped them in the well-scorched cotton cloth, then laid them down to cool.

With ominous deliberation, she screwed the top carefully on the jar of hair grease, and gathering up the combs and brushes she walked calmly out of the kitchen.

The air was thick as a cloud of sizzled hair and undigested pomade floated below the kitchen ceiling resisting all efforts of the little breeze that came through the open windows. I stood speechless staring into the round hand mirror and trying to replay my words.

I looked strange; my image confirmed what I already knew. Parted down the center, one half of my hair was black, sleek , pressed straight and sweeping my shoulder, while the other half jutted out to the side, wiry and stiff like an angry porcupine.

It had started simply. The biweekly ritual of pressing the hair was more stressful than glamorous, and I would actually dread it except that my mother used this time to relate the plot of movies or tell engrossing stories.

She hoped this would make me relax, and not sit in tense anticipation of getting burns on my neck, my ears, or my scalp. The iron stove we used did not modulate the heat; it all depended on my mother's timing, and the cotton cloth on which she wiped each hot comb was her only gauge of its intensity.

Sometimes a great hole would be burned into the cloth, other times a slight brown scorch stain, which would let her know that she needed to set it aside to cool down for a bit before combing my damp oiled hair through its tines.

"Your hair is growing nicely," my mother commended me, as she unloosed the first damp French twists. Right after the shampoo and towel dry, when the hair was damp and easy to comb, she had parted it down the center, made four sections each side and loosely combed and twisted the eight braids.

This was the good part of the experience; before the open air made it dry and stiff, my hair combed easily. I was happy to get compliments for my hair, because of the four sisters my hair was finest and took the longest time to grow and thicken.

It was my mother's many years of diligent cornrow braiding that had finally made it grow.

"So, I can wear it in a pony tail sometimes, like the teenagers, and get bangs." I had continued, already beginning to fantasize that I might resemble American teenagers who were the craze in the movies that everyone was talking about and going to see.

Rock and roll was creeping into the country. "Rock around the Clock", " Rock, Rock, Rock", these were the movies with long lines on weekends and holidays, movies I had only heard about on the radio or from my friends.

I stared longingly at their posters, outside of cinemas on my way home from school, and I knew this was the extent of my engagement with them. There were rules in our house, and these movies were deemed inappropriate, their only purpose to lead the young astray.

My older sister had been allowed to see "Peyton Place", and then my parents had regretted this decision when they later heard what the story was all about.

Biblical spectaculars were the favorites in our house. We had all seen "The Ten Commandments" with Charlton Heston, and "The Robe" with Richard Burton. My mother, however, loved the old lavish ones, the Cecil B. DeMilles', which she could describe with all the attendant sound effects.

I knew every frame of" Samson and Delilah", which I had never seen, but I had shed many tears as my mother described how Victor Mature, shorn of his hair was blinded and enslaved.

Today, she was dramatizing all the action from "Barabbas", hoping to change the subject; but my discontent grew. I wanted to see the modern movies; the ones that my friends talked about at school.

My mother disagreed, she was worried that this teenager craze made children grow up too fast and get into trouble.

"I want to go to the cinema like my friends in school," I insisted.

"And I want to wear my hair nice and look like regular people." I started in when she did not reply.

"Hold your ear," my mother directed," and don't bend down so low."

I had a habit of sliding low in the chair, when I sensed the hot breath of the comb on the back of my neck. I turned down the top of my ear with the fingers of my left hand and continued to argue that I was old enough for a hairstyle that did not make me look like a pickaninny.

She let that pass.

"It's enough to be poor -- I don't need to be poor and strange."

That must have been it. They were sensitive that I was ashamed of my origins because I was at an English school. They often said that my success was proof that brains could take you where money could not, and I knew that my mother who took great pains to have me correctly outfitted at school would take exception at being called poor.

Poverty was of the spirit; there were subtle gradations of tradition and gentility that the unschooled mistook for poverty.

For a brief moment I had forgotten -- earned my mother's cool disdain, and she had abruptly ended her association with my hair.

My first thought was to get the combs hot again, and try my best with the undone half. But my right ear was still smarting from a burn, where the comb nicked me, and the thought of ruining the other ear dismayed me.

I bunched the undone half and attempted to braid it into two while I got my courage up. Looking at the unsatisfactory result, I began to wonder if it was too late to apologize to my mother.

At eleven years old, I understood parental display; if my mother argued and railed, that was approachable anger that I felt I could handle; but when my mother was silent and seething, that spelled danger and I had to let time pass and devise a plan.

The rudeness for which I had missed the opportunity to apologize was a small thing, but the passing of time made it worse. I put my nose in the air and set out to ignore my mother in her own house.

My sister tried to warn me, "Say you are sorry. Go and prostrate yourself. Cry!"

I was the stingiest child with my tears. Not even for a beating, would I let them fall. My eyes would fill up, but my jaw would stay stern and unyielding.

"Dumb insolence" was what my mother called it, and we knew it was a battle of wills, that as a child, I was expected to lose gracefully.

At the time, it seemed most important to hold out; even though I would have to face the humiliating laughter from my school classmates.

I dampened the frizzy part and combed it as close to my head as possible. Then, though the two braids were hopelessly uneven -- the shiny one twice as thin and twice as long as the stubby one -- I tied my black hair ribbons at the tops of the braids and then used bobby pins to secure them across each other just above my ears.

This put the hair above the nape of my neck, out of view, or so I hoped -- way in back.

I could not dream of covering my head in any way, with a cap or beret, because our school uniform was very strict. Hats with two-inch brims worn outdoors were removed immediately upon entering the premises.

Schoolgirls will immediately observe, dissect, comment upon, and ridicule whatever is in the least contrary to their expectations.

So they laughed at my unusual hairdo as expected, and I told my sad tale, or my version of it. Luckily, sympathetic Pat

Moore, eager to be my friend, offered to have her mother finish my hair when I accompanied her home after school.

I was ecstatic.

I had engaged their sympathy with the lie that my mother had sprained her wrist. So it was that I compounded two sins with a third.

In any case, I returned home nicely groomed, but burdened down with the guilt that I was a truly sinful creature and only bad things could come to me.

It was this sense of shame and guilt that led to my tears. I had planned to return home, comb out my tresses and flaunt them before my mother.

"See, see, I don't need you."

I would not need to say the words, my gait and the angle of my proud head would say it all.

Mrs. Moore had asked few questions. She was, in fact, an accomplished hairdresser. She made short work of it and had turned me out looking far sleeker than my mother had ever managed to do. I thanked her profusely and told her how surprised and pleased my mother would be.

But when I returned home, the threat of continued silence and the thought that I was sinking into a morass of sin overwhelmed me and I ran to my mother and cried.

She, poor soul, was willing to forgive and she hugged me so hard that I felt that contests of wills and unhappiness would never be a match for the shelter of my mother's arms.

SWEET TEETH

Two blocks from the Metropole cinema, Sue-a-Quan opened an ice cream shop and soda fountain. They were the same merchants who started the first supermarket a few years back and changed the way people in Guyana did their grocery shopping, and now they were leading the way again into modern teenage culture.

In the newspaper comics, Archie and Jughead drank milkshakes with their dates and in the movies, James Dean and Natalie Wood sipped cokes at soda fountains and fell in love. Could we expect the same excitement in our plain restricted lives now that this new place existed on Robb Street; would this at last turn the abstraction of teenage life in America into reality for us? I dreamed of going to the Metropole for a double feature then to the soda fountain afterwards. It would be a teenage gathering place, we would dance to rock and roll and have adventures and fall in love.

It remained a dream for the most part, because even the simple routine of being invited to a movie was a difficult business: a potential date would have to ask my parent's permission to take me, and then stipulate when exactly I would be back and where in detail we were going.

This minute accounting, undertaken to preserve the reputation of daughters, took all the joy and spontaneity out of social life -- unless one resorted to sneaking out. The teenage life style never happened and the soda fountain closed in less than a year. Sometime before its end, I had gone once with my mother after a show; what I remember and relish until now was the bounty and sheer excess of what it offered.

I had a banana split after taking at least half an hour to absorb and drool over the list of choices. It came on a low oval dish and resembled a portion that would feed our entire family rather than a single serving. There were three scoops covering the banana slices, one each of vanilla, strawberry and chocolate ice cream and then there was hot fudge sauce and chopped nuts to top it off.

Never in my life had I tasted anything as overwhelmingly sensual and luscious as this; it came as a sudden jolt to the frugality of my sense of what perfection or happiness of joy could be.

I had not seen; I had not lived; if all of this was routinely available as part of being alive.

LOST AND FOUND

Miss Barret decided that the final term of fourth form would be country-dances.

We were used to the galloping kind, where we raced in mad frenzy and stomped our feet in the usually sacred assembly hall, swinging our partners with loud whooping sounds. Liberation, an opportunity to act rebellious and loud with permission, and a welcome respite from the restrained demeanor our school expected.

Gym was strenuous and detailed, it freed us to sweat and behave like the animals we truly were. The balance beam, the horse, juggling with clubs, arm strength, marching in formations. You had to concentrate and you had to move.

"Speed it up", she would shout when lazy, lady-like girls succumbed to sloth and we would rouse ourselves and run. We wore green knickers and cotton gym shorts and should have had jersey tops as well, because our blouses became sticky and uncomfortable.

I suppose if there were changing rooms and some means of showering, they might have required these things, but it was relatively easy to exchange our school tunics for shorts and then change back again for our classes, so that was the way they did it then. The sporty students delighted in their physical strength and skill; it was a different testing ground than the mental agony of the classroom.

But Miss Barret meant formal international dances -- nothing raucous; she wanted grace and style and she made us stand straight and walked among us designating who would do the male roles and who the female. The shorter rounder girls would be females, and the taller more loose-limbed, males. We formed sets of four: Lucille and I were paired with Fidele and Hilda, class athletes who could mimic the flair and nonchalance of credible subalterns.

We made our costumes in Domestic Science class. Dark skirts transformed with yards and yards of ric-rac braid, and breeches and vests sewn with ribbons and piping.

Those days, I thought of Hilda as a dashing character. She was a pretty girl with a tiny waist and fine hair, and there was nothing masculine about her, but she was so smooth that you felt she could play any role she wanted. We danced De Woolf from Austria, Konoscka from Russia, the Italian Tarantella and displayed such grace and style that we were costumed guests at the May Day fair for the YWCA. We had our photographs taken and color slides of us mounted as advertisement for our class.

We read Little Women and one of our exercises was to stage a scene from it. My group chose the scene where Mrs. Crocker comes to tea and Jo is trying to impress her though everything is going wrong and Laurie interrupts and makes lighthearted fun of it all.

We chose Hilda to play Laurie; only she could be the dashing, handsome neighborhood boy.

In the days when Elvis was King, rock and roll in all the cinemas and we were fifteen enjoying the confusion of teenage years, rumors began to swirl about Hilda; she was sick for the final term and never came back.

August is a hot month, school is out, time for day outings, for longer trips to visit relatives. Rumor had it that Hilda was pregnant and sent away to relatives, out of the country.

I hoped that by September when life returned to normal, I would see her in class again. It never happened; but I just refused to believe such a thing could happen to someone so suave.

Bishop's code was inviolable, and any scandal was anathema. Bishop's girls must be beyond suspicion; their families models of respectability. There was a time, when regardless of exam score, the daughter of unmarried parents had no hope of entering Bishops, and had to resort to the convent schools. The rules were lightening up, but did not accommodate pregnancy among its pupils.

It was twenty-seven years before I saw Hilda again -- at a Bishops reunion in Toronto. She was the best looking among our classmates, a successful businesswoman, accompanied by her grown daughter. She introduced the young woman to me without the slightest hint of embarrassment, and I realized at once that the old rumors had been true.

Her life had not ended. Despite the hypocrisy of our school, she had come back on track, gained an education, a business and a husband, ironically, the brother of another Bishops girl.

SUDDIE

When I remember Suddie, a country town at the mouth of a river, I recall the pale thin arms of Marguerite as she languished on a settee.

Pale Hands, pink-tipped beside the Shalimar...

Her maid in crisp white apron served us tea and scones. This was the closest I had ever come to the romance I read about in poems and novels:

I will make you brooches and toys for your delight
Of bird-song at morning and star-shine at night
I will make a palace fit for you and me
Of green days in forests and blue days at sea.

Marguerite lived in the Great House; she had married the District Commissioner who administered the territory like a viceroy, but Marguerite had not married for love.

She was the grande dame who broke champagne on the prows of ships, and cut ribbons to open new bridges; she was invited everywhere, to every tea, to every cocktail party of note and it was she who welcomed Princess Margaret Rose to the district, dressed in pale lilac with matching silk gloves.

I saw Marguerite as a tragic figure, languishing in dreary obligation in the midst of luxury and great natural beauty, without love.

The Essequibo coast was a world away from the capital city, Georgetown, where a general strike and political strife raged on. Here my classmate Evelyn and I escaped the stress of the city, the censure of our teachers, and the burden of Bishops.

April 1963. We had come for Easter vacation, a short respite before the trauma of Advanced Level exams and the fierce competition for scholarships to universities abroad. In our final year at Bishops, a few months could decide whether we succeeded or failed forever in our lives.

To add to our mental woes, the entire social system of *the* country was in upheaval. For us, Essequibo seemed at the end of civilization; newspapers rarely interrupted the lazy flow of rural life; there was no threat of food shortage; everyone seemed to grow on their plots exactly what they wanted to eat.

Suddie was the administrative center and the District Commissioner functioned as governor, leading a corps of local functionaries in administering law and services to the region -- the police, courts, hospital, roads and waterways.

These locals had replaced the English colonial administrators and had adopted entirely the decadence of their predecessors: the grand mansions, the maids, the cocktail parties.

Evelyn and I were thrilled to be included; her brother was the district engineer, and his English wife eager to please, placed none of the restrictions on us that any local woman would have put on schoolgirls. What a treat for us.

Away from the scrutiny of parents and schoolteachers, welcomed into an adult world where you could actually make the law for yourself, we are heady and excited by this sudden dose of freedom. At first, we were confused by the myriad of options for laziness and ease.

In those beautiful houses no chores were expected of us; local women came in to cook, to clean, to pick up after us -- buxom country girls who eyed us with suspicion when we crossed the line in our efforts to be friendly by excessively questioning them.

The beach was just outside our door, fresh food from the farms, fruit trees everywhere. We roamed the beaches; we bathed, swam, and walked through villages with pastoral names: Paradise, Aurora, Golden Fleece.

At cocktail parties, the Australian engineers not caring that we are plain schoolgirls flirted with us, so we swilled cocktails and giggled in pretended sophistication.

Late at night, we stood on the verandah and smoked the cigarettes we dutifully collected at these parties; in the seductive silence of night, we contemplated the moon and dreamed. Free from structure and school rules we delighted in the anarchy of the countryside, which our naive eyes mistook for true freedom.

The idyll did not last, the unrest spread and workers in the countryside joined the general strike. When the hospital workers walked off, we volunteered though we feared the horror of disease and the drudgery of boiling dirty sheets.

Dressed in scrubs, we helped instead in the maternity ward and Evelyn, presaging the physician she would become, paraded incredulously through the delivery room when our first infant was born.

We were still stranded on the Essequibo coast when term started. No ferry boats, no sanctioned way to get back to Bishops and exams. News came that a car loaded with explosives was intercepted on Carmichael Street, near the British Council building, across the street from Bishops, and students had to be evacuated. More rumors that Bishops had been bombed, and we saw our future blown away as well.

Until one night, we calmed our terror and decided to leave. Evelyn's brother drove us along the coast to Supernam, there we boarded an overcrowded launch that plied its way across the Essequibo and back to Georgetown.

THE PATRIARCH

She called the child, Boswell, a name she remembered from the Royal Readers she used in school. It was the name of somebody important and her child would grow up to be important, even though they said on his birth certificate: father unknown.

Unknown to them, she mused, because the father did not come with her and sign his name, and she had no marriage certificate to show to the clerk in the government office. Ruby Thomas was a washerwoman in the parish of St Lucy in Barbados. She was an honest hardworking woman, active in her church, and not for a moment did she believe that God disapproved her way of life.

This child of hers with the sugar brown skin, and the soft curly hair was the beloved child of a man of status, a property owner and merchant who had sired only daughters with the wife who put food in front of him and barely looked at him when she did so.

His backra wife was eager to climb into society but she did not love the husband who came to Ruby's cottage for comfort. Ruby knew the rules: stay out of sight, don't push yourself in public, and above all avoid confrontation with his family. She had no fears that he would not take care of her son.

He held the child and looked into its eyes as if he could see in its innocence a miniature of himself. He visited more often since the birth of his child, and would bring, not only money, but toys, a kite, balloons. He had a studio portrait taken of himself with his son, and gave Ruby a copy to keep in a safe place. One day the boy would grow up, claim his heritage, and his father would not be unknown.

Ruby had her child christened in the Anglican Church: Boswell Aloysius Thomas. She used her father's name as the middle name because it was tradition that the middle name be at least three syllables long.

As the boy grew, he would help his mother deliver clean laundry to her clients. He would walk beside her, holding her hand tightly, as she maneuvered along the public road, balancing a tray of starched and pressed clothes on her head. She took long strides in the laced up men's shoes that she wore; she was a big boned country girl, not pretty but energetic and comely.

That was what had attracted Mr. Mendoza to her: her open smile and easy way of conversation. He owned a string of dry goods stores, appearing at one or other of them as he chose, his motive being maximum profit. He made small talk when he saw her, he could relax with her, and there was no guile in her communication. And when she walked away carrying the sack of dirty laundry, he heard in his head the echoes of songs of Solomon,

"Thou art black but comely...thy breasts are like twin does"

He started to give her more groceries than she had paid for, and then he started to visit her.

Now that she came with her son to the grocery shop, the manager he had hired gave her the groceries on account. They understood that this boy was his son, and treated the washerwoman with a certain amount of respect.

The patron had risen above the everyday trade and became a member of the parish council as his wife and daughters moved up in society.

The boy wanted for nothing, went to the Anglican school and was provided whatever lessons he showed a penchant towards. He was good with his hands, but he did not like his books, so at fourteen they apprenticed him to a cooper to learn a trade.

There was a quiet anger in the boy as he grew into adolescence. When he was past the age of toys, his father never talked to him as a son, and the dream his mother had that he would manage the grocery business faded when he chose fishing over school and never passed his examinations.

The mother suffered from swollen ankles but continued with her work: washing, bleaching, bluing, starching, sprinkling, bucking up, and ironing -- tasks that took six days out of every week. She needed the boy to fetch and deliver the clothes now that her legs were giving out, and the patron's goodwill did not extend beyond groceries.

The boy resented the injustice that he saw on his island, and he hated the food his mother put before him. He would cry out and it hurt her to hear him:

"We are getting the scraps from the master's table when I deserve the fatted calf."

Among the men at the cooper's shop, Boswell learned to become a man. He watched and learned the trade; he listened as they talked, and learned about men and women and about life. Then he began to put into practice what he had learned.

At sixteen, he could handle his Friday night cask water as well as the seasoned drunkard, and the boys of his youth looked to him for leadership and began to call him 'Boss'.

Word was that a man could start a new life in British Guiana. Land was going cheap and there was a push for developing the areas around the capital; there was a building boom, tradesmen of all sorts were in demand. Boats were leaving at the end of every month with new explorers. Boss pondered this for a long time, and then he went to talk with his father.

The old man was ailing, he wanted the boy to come see him again, let them talk. But the backra wife, listening in, talked her own story with the youth and encouraged him to go away, start fresh somewhere. Yes, she would help to set him up.

Boss told his mother just two days before he left for B.G. He knew what to expect, two days of weeping, though he promised to come back and take her to live in the house he would build there.

Ruby's son never returned to St. Lucy, but he sent money for her with an uncle who was returning to Barbados. The woman he married, Madge Durant, was the child of other Bajans. Her father was a respected tailor-cutter and her mother, a seamstress, trained girls in her home. He always meant to take Madge home to his mother, to see the place her own parents had come from.

Life moved on swiftly and at the time of the photograph, Boss was the stately patrician, father of his own family, sitting for his formal portrait in his backyard on a Sunday afternoon. My Dada, his oldest daughter, stands on his left.

Far from his thoughts were his mother and the patron, both long dead.

All he could see was a future in the new country, bigger than his small island, with forests and rivers deep within, opening up every day with gold and diamonds.

AUBREY

I am watching Aubrey, his gold front teeth shining through his smile, as he claps the hot roti and stacks them on the plate. He is a cook by profession, but the gold teeth are from his show business life; he has aspirations to be a nightclub singer. Twice he has earned mention on the radio in the Ovaltine Amateur Hour; he knows he has a good voice, but what he needs to win is professional management; someone to choose and arrange the songs that best suit his voice and put flash in his presentation.

He is singing "Stardust" as he works, and his mellow tones are a soothing contrast to the swift, light action of his hands. He grabs a roti hot off the griddle, claps the air bubbles out, pinches it in the center, then shakes it like a handkerchief before folding it to join the stack. Quick, quick, now another one... a white mountain of roti rises before my eyes.

When he was to come on the radio show, he announced it to the whole family and everyone gathered in our house on the Saturday night of the broadcast. We knew he was good, but everyone seemed disappointed that he did not sound as good as he does when he sings at home. He chose a medium tempo song popular at that time, called Slowpoke:

*Why keep me waiting, while it's getting aggravating,
you're a slowpoke*

I wait and worry but you never seem to hurry, you're a
slowpoke
Time means nothing to you, I wait and then, you're
late again...
Eight o'clock, nine o'clock quarter to ten...

We all could sing along, and we did as we listened, but Aubrey sounded so lifeless we were not surprised that he lost to a spunkier singer.

The consolation was a carton of Ovaltine products that we knew would end up at our house for everyone to enjoy.

My uncle told him he should choose better songs, more spirited songs, but Aubrey insisted that only the professional stamp of training abroad would set him right.

He watches movies with Frank Sinatra or Sammy Davis singing, and believes he could be in that very league. He is a good fellow; he has been working at catering jobs to pay for voice lessons and to save for his passage to America.

But he is not obsessive or penny pinching, he likes to dress well and he is generous; whenever he has a stroke of good luck, or if he gets a raise in his job, he always does something extra kind. Usually he buys a gift for his mother or grandmother; but lately he has been studying and thinking about his future, so he is reaching outwards. Cast your bread upon the waters and it will return after many days. Today he is feeding the poor.

They come on a bus. He has paid the driver to pick up ten people from Archer Poor Home and ten people from the Dharam Sala. He is balancing his generosity to include both the black and Indian poor of his country. The food he has prepared is also true to this philosophy: he made roti and vegetable curry but he has also cooked a pot of rice and peas with salt pork.

He has accepted the help of his mother and grandmother and they are in the kitchen serving up the plates of food while he stands outside to welcome each guest and seat them down around the table under the mango tree. On each side, there is a basin of water and a clean towel for people to wash their hands, before he asks them to bow their heads for giving thanks. His prayer is short:

"Thank thee merciful father for this food for the nourishment of our bodies, Amen."

He looks so young, moving among the mottled mass of beggars, and I look from the window as the noise level increases and food disappears off their plates. Somebody has asked if there is any rum, but Aubrey is strict and will serve only water and mauby.

He knew what was right, a moral sense is what we call it, yet why did life treat him so? I think they never forgave me for not showing up when he died. So much had happened in between, sometimes I was right there but who really cares at the end. It makes the regret pile up so it drowns any other feelings and the bile rises in my throat so I become hoarse without explanation for weeks at a time.

Better to avoid all that and look back at the bits and pieces that we stitch together as our only legacy. I was there that early morning at the Church of the Nazarene when Aubrey married the Lutchman girl. She was a small-built round-faced red girl, and her father high in the church. Only relatives were there: the bride's people on the right side of the aisle and the groom's on the left.

His brother was away at Bible College, and could not be his best man. A friend in a morning coat stood up with him, but it was a hurry wedding, very early in the morning, because the girl was showing already, and she a minister's daughter.

There was organ music and Aubrey's voice ringing out as the sun rose, in an anthem to his bride: O Promise Me. Framed in the morning light from the stained glass windows, Aubrey looked out onto the relatives, and sang as if his life depended on this truth he was telling us all:

> *O promise me that someday you and I*
> *will take our love together to some sky,*
> *where we can be alone and faith renewed*
> *we'll find a place where sweet flowers bloom...*

It brought tears to my eyes; I thought it was the most romantic moment I had ever lived, and could not understand how his mother could suck her teeth and call him foolish.

It was years later, when the marriage was no marriage and everybody knew about it, and the baby was born, that I understood. Aubrey had never lived one day with her. It was a kindness, he explained, after she had run off to Canada with some older man who promised her a good life.

As far as we knew, Aubrey did not have any other girl friend but he always looked good and happy when he came to visit, and he was still keeping up his singing.

Then the frolics started appearing in the newspapers: the weddings where men dressed as women played all the roles of bride and bridesmaids, dressed with elaborate trains of silk and satin, and danced together in ceremonies that took over the best hotels and dance halls.

The word got out and crowds would line up to see and the gossip would spread; and more than one person had seen Aubrey as bridesmaid and even bride, and they had pictures of him in his costumes as proof.

We did not go near Waterloo Street, where the auntie- men frolics ended up in brawls. Once a relative saw Aubrey on a ferryboat at a dance and she recognized him but told him not to talk to her when he was with "those people".

Though I lost touch with his life, I knew he came to America and joined a church and was a soloist. I saw him again when much time had passed, when he was older and lived with his mother in Brooklyn.

I drove my mother there one night; Aubrey brought out his Bristol Cream Sherry and we toasted, and I promised to come back another day and hear about his life. All we did was present my husband and children, exchange a few platitudes about life, not knowing that was the last time.

Next, we heard he was ill in hospital but I did not accompany my mother to visit him. When they moved him to a hospice he asked her not to come; he did not want anyone to see him. His brother took weeks out of his life and came and tended him; washed him and shaved him and was with him in his death.

This is less Aubrey's story than my effort to understand my own life and what family and relations mean as one grows in the wider world from childhood to adult life.

LOVERS AND MADMEN

One band of shame across the family tree was Ivan with his shoes in his hand, ready to run if he heard the wail of a siren or spied a policeman's blue from the corner of his eye. He would show up suddenly at our house, bathed in so much sweat that the tight curls on his head glistened and rivulets poured from his temples. His tattered shirt stuck to his back and he smelt bad. That was why Victor kicked him when he appeared at our back door. And Ivan, a grown man kicked him right back. We were dumfounded. Here was my four-year-old brother, holding his knee and bawling in anger and pain and Ivan just standing there unruffled:

"Mommy, he kick me," Victor screamed, throwing himself down on the floor for emphasis, while Ivan countered with calm rationality:

"Tit for tat, little fellow, see how you like that!"

The real commotion began when my father appeared. My mother would have settled everything fine, but my father had a way of exaggerating and the sight of Ivan only aggravated him.

"What are you doing here, disrupting my house?"

Victor's crying was now tremendous, and he clung to my father's legs, crying:

"Daddy, daddy,… he kick me."

And my father spread his arms dramatically and lifted his eyes to whatever higher power he expected to judge this:

"This man is stark, raving mad and getting madder…who knows what he will do next? Why doesn't he go beg somewhere else. Get him to hell out of here!"

My mother always had a soft spot for Ivan, and here she was trying to keep things quiet, acting the peacemaker, opening the door wide, trying to lure Ivan inside for something to drink. We stood near the door, holding back, watching to see what would happen next. This angered my father even more and he began to shout as if he was the one who was mad. He railed on, flaying his arms out towards Ivan:

"You set foot in here and I will break your damn neck! Or better yet, I will call the police!"

Ivan stared as if dealt a blow. His eyes widened in terror. He looked beyond my father, did not hear anything except Police! Then, fast and sudden, he bolted. My mother stood there with the cream soda bottle in one hand and the opener that she had just taken the cap off with, in the other; she just stood there with her mouth open, looking stupid.

We used to keep Ivan's suitcase, an old battered cardboard grip pale brown with dark brown corners. He had come and left it in our cupboard for safe keeping, and from time to time, he would show up to retrieve clean clothes or get other things that he needed out of it. Otherwise, he lived wherever, on the street, and we supposed, certainly, on the run. He kept his shoes off to run faster in his bare feet and outrun whichever constable would chase him; this obsession turned him into a barefoot bum.

Before he went off his head, he was one of Sadler's best bakers, and got bread even now from them. In fact, old man Sadler refused to believe he was mad, just thought he was going through tough times. He understood, he said, with a wife like that, who could blame Ivan? He told Ivan that when things worked themselves out he could come back to his job at the bakery.

Things never got worked out, and Ivan never held a job again in his life.

What had come over his mind that day was surely madness. He was not even drunk. He never believed himself to be a cruel man, but what he had done that night was unforgivable. It was as if a dam had broken and a man he did not know had completely lost himself in knocking the senses out of his wife. She ended up in hospital and he, forever running from the law. He ran away when the ambulance came, the sirens still sounding in his ears and completely forgot about their children, the twin sons who were his pride and joy.

The neighbors must have taken them in until the relatives took over. He had returned late one night and in the dark, avoiding the neighbors, he slunk into the house and got his belongings out in his suitcase. Pots and pans still strewn on the kitchen floor from their fight, the place looked empty and sad.

He never asked how badly she was hurt and he never went to the hospital to find out; he only heard that they had set the police on him. He thought he would get on a boat and go into the bush for a few months or a few years, but he could not move himself to action. He hid out down by the race course for how many days he could not remember, not eating, not even sleeping, just feeling bad. One day it did not matter anymore, the only important thing was to stay ahead of the police.

My Aunt Glenda had married Ivan when everyone thought she would remain single all her life. She was thirty; living with her mother and working at the new shirt factory. She helped in the house and was active in her church choir, and because she worked for her own money, she dressed well and went to the cinema often with her women friends from work. She was a woman accustomed to doing as she pleased, and for years now had not bothered with the kinds of boyfriends who came courting without a pot to piss in.

How Ivan had charmed her into taking an interest in him, was a puzzle to everyone. All of a sudden, he came courting with a lot of good humor and hot, fresh tennis rolls from the bakery where he worked, and the family began to like him. He was handsome and very muscular and there were unembarrassed squeals of delight when Glenda said goodnight to him in the dark. He had managed to open up whatever romantic vein she had been preserving under her brusque exterior, she blossomed into radiance, and everyone said marriage agreed with her.

If my Aunt Glenda had listened, she would never have married Ivan. Nennie always said the two things you do not want to find in your mate's family history are madness and cocobeh. People with cocobeh are easy to spot: you look to see if their fingers and toes cramp inwards. It is just a matter of time before fingers and toes start dropping off, and the victim banished to the leprosy colony at Mahaica.

Madness, however, could lie dormant until something set it off, like Ivan, so you had to listen and judge all rumors that you heard.

They said Ivan's mother had refused to let the midwife take her stillborn child and sat holding her dead baby in her arms. When her husband wrestled it away and buried it, she sat silent for months and never spoke to him again. She was strange, they say, gone mad, and people sympathized with her husband when he took another woman and had a brand new family. Aunt Glenda must have heard all of this as a faint background noise against the reality of strong, handsome Ivan, with his plan to open his own bakery and provide her with her own home and family.

Aunt Glenda and Ivan were happy. We looked forward to their visits to our house as much for the fun as for the ample supply of butter flaps, tennis rolls and aniseed biscuits they always brought. They were making plans to move to Buxton village where Ivan grew up and open their bakery there with their savings. Aunt Glenda was learning to bake, and getting excited about how prosperous they would be. They worked hard and saved; no more cinema dates, their only trip was church, and Ivan was always with his wife. On more than one occasion, I heard my father say:

"Glenda got to give that man breathing space; she won't let him out of her sight: just work and church, he can't even have a drink with his friends. All work and no play make Jack a dull boy. Glenda thinks she can take a man like if he is bread dough and mold him into a mouse!"

My aunt stopped working at the factory when she became pregnant with the twins and their plans to move stalled, and we noticed how cross and sarcastic she was becoming. She began to criticize her husband to her friends and put all her attention on her babies, erasing Ivan from her consciousness.

We did not enjoy their visits anymore and they came separately, Ivan to seek sympathy from my mother and Aunt

Glenda, with the babies in tow, to complain about what a useless man Ivan was and how he had ruined her life.

Then the big blowup when Ivan lost control. After her hospital stay, Glenda went back to live with her mother, then started her job again while my grandmother cared the boys.

Ivan joined the parade of eccentric characters that streamed through the idle days of my childhood. We chased them down the streets, shouting their nicknames and taunting them: Uncle Cato, Walker the Nigger, Jingle Bells!

Some were harmless sources of humor and teasing them took the boredom out of a schoolchild's life, but others were dangerous and threw stones or terrified children with their curses. Red eyed and desperate, mumbling to themselves, or railing out against an unfair sky, mad people served as cautionary tales against excess and sins of pride, and children were supposed to take heed.

We never denied that Ivan was our relative, everyone knew he was; we were just grateful that he was a low-keyed madman and that he stayed away from the schools we attended.

The police complaint against him must have lapsed a long time ago, but this knowledge never penetrated Ivan's certainty that he was a wanted man. He never stayed long in any place; never let you know when to expect him. He became old quickly, it seemed, and kept losing more of his teeth every time we saw him, and these times stretched further and further apart.

Until one day, my father in a fit of anger threw Ivan's suitcase out. All it contained was a few rags and many old shoes.

POLYDORE

He was tall and spare with a face as contained and severe as an ebonite carving and he moved with the unhurried silent arrogance guaranteed to exasperate righteous people like Aunt Cil.

"He can fool the rest of you," she exclaimed, "but if he doesn't pay my rent, I shall throw him into the street."

Polydore had the audacity to be late with the rent without excuse or plea for pity, and he had placed two posters with his picture and the caption under it saying "Proprietor", on the outside wall of the cottage, near the front door. The posters were leftovers from the days when he owned a dry goods shop, before they put him in jail for fraud and larceny. Though his circumstances had changed, he was not the man to accept that he had come down in the world.

He was well-spoken, with an educated English vocabulary that never descended to vernacular when he bothered to answer anyone's queries. He never left the house without a necktie and when dressed, he wore long sleeved shirts with cufflinks. I say when dressed, because Polydore observed his own peculiar dress code: inside his house, he and his wife wore not a stitch of clothing. really?

This came as a shock the first time a neighbor knocked at his door and he appeared. Once we knew that this was no isolated incident, everyone understood that if his nudity offended you, then you had to wait until you saw him outdoors to deal with him. This presented a dilemma for Aunt Cil, a proper, church-going woman who as his aggrieved landlord, had publicly announced that she was going in there to reclaim her property. Undaunted by reports of his nudity, she knocked at his door and announced:

"Make yourself decent, Mr. Polydore. I am here to see you on business."

"I am coming", he responded.

She turned her back to his door and faced the audience of yard folk who were at their doors to witness the drama. They laughed uproariously, making remarks about his coming.

Then Polydore opened the door and shouted:

"Boo!!!"

Aunt Cil was halfway down the stairs in fright before she realized that he was there in a teasing mood dressed in a robe like an African Prince and laughing for all he was worth.

I cannot recall what lured her into accepting him as a tenant in the first place; she knew of his disgrace because, in the past, she patronized his store and knew the whole story of the sixteen-year-old girl who was his shop assistant before he got her pregnant and made her his second wife.

There was also a time when he dabbled in politics; he had been a candidate with one of the conservative parties that had sprung up suddenly with the coming of universal adult suffrage. This was a heady time, a time of sudden political education and awareness. Everyone, not only property owners, could now vote for their government, and everyone's vocabulary became inflated with talk of rallies, manifestoes, imperialism and propaganda. Posters of political candidates were plastered on every available wall and tree trunk and Polydore's was among them. He had been a rabid anti-communist.

My aunts feared that the communists would take the roof from over their heads and give away the property that their dear papa had left them to the hordes of lazy tenants that owned nothing and never worked to own anything.

The progressives, they distrusted too. They would wake them early in the morning and set them out on the estates to cut cane in the boiling sun. Yes, even the old folks; if you were deemed too old to work, you would be deemed too old to eat and put outdoors to starve and die.

Parents dragged their children to nightly meetings at Bourda Green. We would have to do our homework by flashlight on soda cartons as we sat on the ground listening to lesser speakers warm up the platform for the political stars. Mr. Polydore was never a star but people remembered him.

163

Perhaps Aunt Cil thought Lot 10 deserved a celebrity, even a failed one, or perhaps her good nature led her to help someone fallen on bad times. By now, Polydore and his wife had four children, named for famous people: Carlyle, Milton, Elizabeth and Victoria. He had his own particular regimen for his children; he took charge of their education and they seldom came outdoors to play. My chief recollection is of them staring longingly at us from the windows of their prison.

We, children, were forbidden to go inside their house, or even to appear ₍at₎ their door. My father said, in no uncertain terms:

"If you're playing with a ball and it goes inside Polydore's house, let it stay there and I will buy you another ball."

My mother was friendly with Doris, Polypore's wife, and she made a point of running over to visit when she observed that Polydore had gone out.

We found out that their children called them full-mouth, by their names: Polydore and Doris, and they had a lot of books and board games in their house. My mother would return home laden with novels that Doris had given her.

"And is she naked when he is not there? And are the children all naked too?"

We were eager to satisfy our constant bewilderment.

"Yes, of course," my mother replied, "They are smart. They don't have to waste money buying all these clothes that you children outgrow so fast." I did not know if she was joking and I tried to imagine how I would fit in a household such as theirs.

My mother thought Doris should get out more and invited her to the Young Marrieds Club. Doris was enthusiastic and wanted to join but Polydore would not even let her go back a second time.

It was clear that everyone was afraid of Polydore and I watched him every opportunity I got -- to see if I could find out what it was in him that everyone feared. He was not a large or muscular man; my father could lick him any day, as could my Uncle Rudolf who was small, but fierce when drunk.

In the year that Polydore was our neighbor, his seething malevolence pervaded the yard. He never raised his voice, but many a night, everyone heard the loud thuds and piteous whimpering as Polydore disciplined his wife and children for some infraction real or imagined. He ruled with an iron fist.

Aunt Cil managed to get rid of Polydore when she deeded the cottage to her nephew and his family. Served with legal papers, he packed up and left. And so, to everyone's relief, Polydore moved on into the anonymity of the world outside Alberttown.

GEM

She hung out the washing, scrubbed the floor of the little garden apartment until the boards gleamed white and clean as a counter top, then sent the little girl out to call Nurse Rose. It was getting harder; she felt pain in her joints and a constant dull ache that knew no exact location.

This is what getting old feels like. I am losing my touch.

She sat on the chair in the kitchen and waited for the kettle to boil. Then she tottered over to the cupboard for the jar of sugar. She reached for the dried toya and mint herbs strung like wilted bridal bouquets from a nail on the hearth, crushed some leaves into a cup and added boiling water, then she stirred in two heaping spoonfuls of Demarara brown sugar. The herbs would soothe her, she was going to need all her strength; this was child number five.

When she had become pregnant the first time, she was sixteen. After her mother had gotten over the shock that that little Gem was doing more with boys than just hiding her face shyly when they whistled and called out as she walked home from school, she took her in hand and shepherded her through the whole thing. Gem had not been afraid; her mother made her drink cod liver oil so that the baby's limbs would be straight and strong, then near the end, she started the regimen of okra soup so that the child would slide out easily and not rip away her taut young insides.

Her mother was dead now; she had helped raise the children, but barely lived past child number three. By the fourth child, Gem's body was on automatic delivery. She never gained much weight; tiny and skinny little Gem, just the big belly out front.

"When are you going to stop? ", a friend from her schooldays asked when she met Gem in the Bourda market. Gem's oldest daughter, taller than her mother already, was holding the shopping basket dutifully while her mother haggled with vendors over the price of vegetables. The friend had touched Gem's stomach as she spoke, and Gem looked up at her, holding her back straight and so pleased with herself that her eyes twinkled:

"I love children, and the Lord gives them to me," Gem said simply, breaking into a dimpled smile.

"Looks like a boy, you are carrying low," her friend commented wisely, but she could see how tattered and poor Gem looked, despite her exuberance, so she offered to help.

"No I am all right," countered Gem, "I have got a good fellow now. This baby's father will take care of me and the children."

Her friend had heard that line before and wished Gem better luck this time.

Gem's fourth child had a real English perambulator, which everyone admired when she sat with her children taking in the afternoon breeze on the sea wall. Her fellow had steady work as a tally clerk at the Rice Marketing Board, a real step up from the men she was accustomed to, one who wore a white shirt and starched collar and carried a pen in his pocket; though he worked on the wharves, he never had to lift anything nor get his hands dirty.

He was the one who put in a good word with the bosses for the brutish sweating stevedores who watched him cautiously with envy and with hate. After the baby son was born, Gem tried to live to a certain standard to fit her man's expectations. He was not overly generous; his only blast of expansiveness was the pram when the baby came. They stayed on, in the same cramped rooms in the yard, and to keep herself decent, Gem tried her hand at raising chickens and selling eggs for extra money. She also did a bit of sewing.

Gem was not a trained seamstress; she had had to leave school before she completed the domestic science program that would have got her into the Carnegie Trade School. She was quick though and could pick up ideas fast, so when her mother died and she inherited the sewing machine, she advertised herself as a seamstress. Nothing complicated; children's clothes and she used her own brood to practice on, making sure that she always put them out in attractive colors. When she dressed them up for band concerts and strolls on the seawall, people would notice and say admiringly:

"I have never seen that style before; how practical, how pretty."

They would come with their yards of material and ask Gem to sew the same style for their child. She was truly creative; some of the ideas came in her dreams and she would spread a great sheet of brown wrapping paper on the kitchen floor and try cutting this way and that until she finally got it right. Her most successful idea was the pants for her little boy. He wanted his pants to have a fly like his father's; at a time when most trousers for small boys had elastic waist and you had to pull them down over their bottoms when they needed to go. She invented the fake fly with the gap under the flap, so that her little man could wiggle his little Willie out when he needed and have exactly the same action as a grownup.

The children were a delight for Gem; she pampered them and sometimes seemed to become a child again in their company. She always made a big fuss for their birthdays; and did so whether or not she had steady money coming in. Mr. Mack at the sweet shop had a juke box that he hired out for parties, toting it over in a little wagon, and bringing records that children would like and also all the latest calypsos that featured in the Trinidad Carnival road march.

Gem's parties were special; the adults had even more fun than the children. The mothers would come and stay, serving the food and helping to control the children. They would gossip amongst themselves; but best of all, the women would dance with each other, free and uninhibited without censure from their men. Spared the lechery of men's eyes when they folded their skirts in between their thighs, they wined down in ecstasy. They would sing along with Sparrow, loud, and raucous and saucy, and wink their eyes and shout all the rude and sexy lyrics.

Gem smiled as she remembered:

"Madeline, sweet, sweet Madeline, tell me where you get that bundle from? ..."

Oh yes, they all knew well enough, bundle after bundle came after the fun done! Every calypso advised women on how to keep their man wanting more. This was her life, whichever man wanted her and treated her good, for a time. Did life hold anything else for her? Was there a world outside this life? Strange thoughts and the spasms that came frequently, made her feel even more tired; this was definitely going to be her last child. She hoped Nurse Rose was on her way.

Nurse Bernice Rose had come to town and taken the house at the corner of First and Light Streets. She was not a local girl returned home, nobody remembered her growing up, yet she always said she was from just around here.

It was a pretty cottage, Victorian carved eaves along a peaked roof, and a row of double sash glass windows along the front and sides. Painted white with a red front door, the red picked up again in the trim just below the gutters along the roof edge

-- a fine bright house in which to start her business as a nurse midwife.

When her sign went up:

Nurse Midwife and Family Planning,

There was no fuss because everyone knew what midwives were for and since people did not believe that families could be planned the remaining words attracted little attention.

That was until the preachers began to put Nurse Rose's name into their Sunday sermons:

"The Lord giveth and the Lord taketh away...

Who is man to tamper with God?

Who is this woman, to tamper with the sacredness of motherhood?

Why should this woman make her house a gathering place for women to sin against God?"

So the first stone was cast, and the glass windows of her house were shattered and Nurse Rose took down her sign.

Nurse Rose did not go away, and the years passed and women began to understand that their bodies were more than vessels for men to drain their sperm into and for babies to tear apart.

Women knew but never discussed with their men the things they worried about among themselves. Perhaps they were doing the men a favor, saving them from having to make decisions, from having to face the inconsistencies of their actions.

The women would talk together as they sat at their door mouths picking rice, sorting the good white grains from the broken and blackened bits.

To put something presentable on the table for the noon meal was a laborious undertaking in homes without refrigerators -- every day a trip to the market, and at home, the fight to salvage food from insects and vermin.

Gem's friend Liza had announced, "My man does not want me to have anything to do with Nurse Rose."

And the other women who had been thankful to Nurse Rose on so many occasions felt sorry for Liza, whose misfortune was frequent miscarriages.

"I am going to the Government clinic to see a real doctor, Liza continued proudly, and I am going to have my child in a hospital."

"Uh,hmm, ..." they muttered in tentative agreement., They wished Liza well; she could not hold on to a baby; so many times it had washed away in a sea of blood before she even showed. The hospital cost a lot of money, and the very idea of it filled them all with dread. They associated the hospital with grievous illness and death.

Yderl had an experience there, so she countered, "They do it wrong at the hospital. My baby was stillborn they told me. But I know it was the long labor that killed my child. They kept me there in pain till it was convenient for them, for their doctor…"

There was so much bitterness in her voice as she recalled, "Twenty hours of hell, and all the time the cord was strangling my child."

It was not that midwives did not sometimes lose babies, but they came when you sent for them, and they stayed to comfort you, and they set you down on your own clean sheets, and you did not die from lying in fever. You died only if you were tired and your time had come.

"And don't expect anything from the men", they cautioned each other.

"My man does not want any barriers to his pleasure", Liza was fond of saying, and the rest of them laughed knowingly. After all, what kind of man would go into a store and buy French letters?

They slapped their knees and laughed uproariously at the notion of such a thing.

Better to go early to Nurse Rose when trouble hit. She was safe and she did not just take your word about how far along you were. A woman with so many everyday problems could get mixed up, or simply forget, so she did not judge or assign blame.

Nurse Rose would first examine with her hand and then calculate, only then would she use her catheter. She knew her stuff; her patients did not end up in the "slipped and fell" ward of the hospital dying of septicemia.

Nine months while they breast fed one child was the only safety the women could count on, after that they were gone again until their bodies cried, "Enough!"

Then they tied their heads with a cloth, sat down in a chair at thirty-five with their legs veined and swollen, and accepted old age.

Let the man run with anything he could keep up with, they smiled with resignation when gossips reported their man's unfaithfulness. It is enough that he comes home and gives me money to cook his food and wash his clothes. He leaves me alone; he is too tired after his wandering, to bother me when he comes home. What more do I want? Let him run, as long as he comes home when he is done!

This was not Gem's life, but it might well have been. The fifth child was her last because Nurse Rose tied her tubes. It was not easy for Gem.

"What use am I now, not yet thirty, like an orange rind, tossed aside with all its usefulness squeezed out, what do I become now?"

Nurse Rose was firm "Do you want to die? And then who will take care of your children?"

Gem turned her face to the wall and for a moment she hated Nurse Rose, a woman who had no children to show for herself, a woman like a man, alone and serious, living her life without a man's protection.

But Gem was frightened by her own frailty this time; with the other babies she had been able to leap off the bed, and be outside hanging the washed birthing cloths on the line, just hours afterwards.

Gem had not discussed any of this with her man; lately he had been complaining about the number of mouths he had to feed. In any case, he never sat and talked but disappeared into the night after he had eaten his meal. When he returned, it was Gem's body, smooth and round in the dark that he craved, not the details of how it functioned.

Gem remained weak for a longer time with this last boy, and the women in the yard looked in on her and took care of her young ones. Joyce, her oldest girl was her mainstay.

Gem looked from her bed as little Joyce boiled water for her, washed baby clothes, cooked food for the tally clerk who was not her father. Gem watched her daughter, barely twelve, the buds of her sprouting breasts poking through her thin cotton dress. She was so unaware, this child on the brink of becoming a woman. Gem began to cry.

"Why are you crying mother, are you in pain? Shall I call Nurse Rose?"

"No, no," Gem shook her head. "I am so lucky to have you, Joyce, I am just emotional, nothing is wrong. I am sorry I have to take you out of school, away from your lessons to help me…"

Joyce was folding the cloth that would bind the protruding navel of her newborn brother. She had already wiped him down and sprinkled Mennen's baby powder between the wrinkled folds of his flesh to prevent chafing.

She moved with such innocent authority.

Gem stared in amazement as if she had a vision, and the tears flooded again:

"I want a different life for you, Joycie, not a life like mine…"

DISPENSER

The first thing he bought himself was a gold watch. That would set the standard for the life he wanted; nothing second-class, only the best. He was still living at home in those days; he had no problems with saving on rent and food. Mother D was happy to have at least one boy child home, she was happy to do for him; she always said it, smiling with delight as he gobbled down the dinner she kept waiting for whenever he showed up.

Being a dispenser was a good steady job, with a certain amount of status; people asked his advice about what to mix with their cod liver oil to keep themselves free from colds, and what was the best thing to mix with Vaseline to keep away annoyances like dandruff. They respected the fact that he had to be a learned person to understand the prescriptions and whatever it was in Latin that doctors sent to the hospital dispensary. He was always helpful and friendly not hoggish or impatient like some of the other fellows there. In truth, he was satisfied with himself; all the clutter, noise and inefficiency of his workplace never touched him, because he had dreams and he could bide his time until the right moment to realize them.

When he had washed down the stewed vegetables and meat his mother had prepared with a beer, he pulled back the kitchen curtain and stared out at the glorious mango tree that graced their property.

"You could never starve here", he said, "This is God's own country."

His family owned two large properties, from the corner all the way to the alley that divided the block. The houses on their land were well-maintained and substantial, three of them occupied by kin, and the rest bringing in good rent. There were fruit trees in abundance: star apple and tamarind in front with the mango, and wonderful abundance of breadfruit and jamoon in back. They had sold the produce to vendors who would then make their living selling the fruit in season in the city markets. In addition, his mother had fenced off a section as her vegetable garden and grew herbs and nearly everything else that she needed for her pot. She didn't mind sharing with her neighbors but most of the time she fretted that if she could busy herself and grow stuff, why couldn't they? She had no patience with lazy people.

As Hal watched idly across the way, he could see the young daughter of the neighbors wheeling her bicycle into the yard. She had just started high school, must be about fourteen, and she was smiling to herself as if she was engaged in some private conversation. Her school bag laden with books was almost toppling off the back but she was in her own world and as he watched her fresh young face, he made his decision. Here was the innocence he could nurture; she would become a part of his dream.

Of course, she looked down when he talked to her, that was the proper way for modest young girls to behave, and it would never occur to her that a grown man, a dispenser, would have any real interest in her. He helped her pump air into her tires one day, assuring her that if she were late for school she could call upon him to vouch for her. She was grateful, and he asked her about her favorite subjects and offered to lend her books if she needed science references. She was happy to have a grown up friend… he even asked her about boyfriends and she blushed shyly.

He could never be sure what she looked like in those days, whether she was what you would call pretty with a cute nose or if her hair was long. He knew for sure it was not sexual because she had hardly filled out and if she did, her baggy school uniform did not highlight budding breasts. She had good sturdy legs with solid calves from all that bicycling and her skin glistened with youthful energy.

Above all, she was potential; very early he knew what she could become if she were saved from the foolishness and falsity that so many women adopted. He had seen how life had spoiled his three sisters, how they had changed in order to get and keep the kind of husbands available for life in that place. He also knew what women without husbands were all about, he was an expert by now on both types of women, and the woman for him would be completely different.

Some years later, people would say that theirs was a marriage made in heaven. She was a success as a medical doctor, but more than that, she had been able to use political astuteness to become a Health Commissioner and a member of important committees and boards that made decisions for the government and international agencies.

She had respect, and innumerable perquisites like first class international travel and tickets to World Cup games, which were really for her husband's enjoyment.

He stood in the background, a senior civil servant with the Prime Minister's ear, and everyone understood the source of her power.

THREE JIMMYS

What kind of woman would name two children, her two sons born a decade apart, exactly the same name? Both were alive though living in different countries. Perhaps she considered one dead, lost forever, so that the second child was a sort of replacement for the first. When I think of it this way, the image of Aunt Irene softens, her action seems reasonable and she gains my sympathy.

From the stories told about her, Aunt Irene was far from soft or loving; she was always the grasping, self-centered one. Her two sisters, the ones left behind, were grateful for every crumb she sent from America, though they never knew when to expect anything, and years would go by without a word from her.

Irene left BG in 1922 and did not return until 1958. She left her two boys, James and Carl, aged five and three in the care of their godparents, and asked her sister Aunt Cil to keep an eye on them. Irene wrote eagerly at first, then intermittently but Aunt Cil made sure that whatever came from America she shared with the boys, even after they had grown into resentful men.

James was the older one, named for his father, but his aunts preferred to call him Rudolf, the name his godparents had contributed. This was fortunate especially since Irene named her third son, born ten years later in America, Jimmy, and soon after that cut the link with the folks at home.

In those days going to America meant a grand ship sailing for three weeks. They went first to Philadelphia because Jimmy, the husband, had musician friends who promised him a job. They settled into a tiny apartment in a rundown black district, and soon Jimmy was playing gigs, sometimes out of town. Irene was devastated.

This America was far below her expectations she could not bring herself to write home, she felt so ashamed. To escape the musty apartment, she found a factory job like most of the musician's wives. She did not care for the women she met, they dressed cheap and floozy-like, seemed so loud and common always shrieking with that awful nasal accent. She had to admit, though, they took life easy. They laughed a lot and were so genuinely friendly that Irene soon fell in with them.

She wanted them to know that Jimmy had been a sergeant major in the BG militia band that played classical concerts in the botanical gardens, attended by the governor and once even by the visiting Prince of Wales. Her children had a nanny and in the afternoons, they were dressed, like Little Lord Fauntleroy, and taken out for walks and band concerts in the gazebos of the gardens and on the seawall.

She wanted to let them know that the tropics were not jungles-- she came from a home that had culture. Her father had substance and that she and her sisters had someone come in to give them piano lessons, and they had a servant to clean their house. She never said a word about these things to the Americans, of course, because she did not want them to call her uppity and shun her, and besides, if she had learned her lessons well, bragging and good breeding were not compatible.

She often thought about her life back home as if to bolster herself against the bleak, cruel city where the people about her acted as if they accepted the notion of their own worthlessness. She knew women who worked in white women's houses, cleaning or doing laundry and the stories they told made her rule out housework for herself. Jimmy would never tolerate that. He was having a great time in the clubs; they liked him and ate up his stuff, all so new and different. They were even going to cut records.

She began to notice that Jimmy was buying new suits, even though the money his music brought in was not half what they expected. He had always been a smart dresser, he could appreciate custom tailoring because he always had fine English cut suits. He loved to display his cufflinks and cigarette case made of 18- carat BG gold, he had brought with him, and he offered the finest rum when any of his mates stopped by.

It was in these early years that Irene decided that with the money they had saved they should send for the boys and begin a serious family life. If factory work was what it took, she was prepared to do two shifts, and her brother who had deserted their father, joined the war and ended up in Tuskegee, had gotten in touch with her and offered to help. So in April of 1925, nearly three years after they had left, Jimmy returned to bring their sons to America.

The boys were now in the care of the aunts and grandfather in the family house at Lot 10. After a year had passed, their godparents deposited them unceremoniously with their suitcases one Sunday afternoon. To this household their father rolled in like a whirlwind with presents and toys. He had brought them new clothes, tweed coats with matching caps because they would be returning to spring weather, which was a whole lot cooler than the tropics.

In their kindergarten classes, Teacher Bourne pointed out America on the globe, and New York where the ship would dock first before they went on to Philadelphia.

Rudolf and Carl brought candy to share, and their toys to show, and Teacher Bourne stood them in front at the assembly and the other children sang farewell and gave them a book where every child had drawn a picture. Their little fatherless cousin Sonny, who also lived with the aunts, recalls how he envied them; he was so near to all of this yet none of it was for him. He always had lived at Lot 10, had never known a father's attention, only the strict discipline of his grandfather. He did not sing, he did not eat his piece of candy, he saved it in the pocket of his shorts and watched his two cousins dressed in their new caps and coat and pantaloons, already looking different from the other children, already American.

Aunt Cil could not pin Jimmy down. She was fretting, she did not know what arrangement Jimmy had made, what was the exact date that their passage was booked for, what particular items she should send up with the boys. Her sister, Margaret, was busy cooking guava jelly and guava cheese, setting out chutney and spices, all the things she was sure her sister Irene would appreciate because she had missed them these many years.

The grandfather, Sir Carrie, wanted nothing to do with the whole business, he did not care for his son-in-law; he said at the start that Jimmy was not to be trusted.

Jimmy played with the BG militia band one afternoon. His saxophone solo was a tremendous success, lauded in the local newspaper, which had a whole paragraph about his success in America.

He was enjoying the homecoming, he slept late, dressed himself smartly and was out every night, sitting in with the band at some of the best hotels, and doing his best to evade the aunts. When they found out the sailing date, the truth came out. He had drunk and sported away the money and had never bought passage for the boys.

"Next time!" was all he said, and without explaining or saying goodbye to his sons, he returned alone. Perhaps his wife was inconsolable, but only for a time since she obviously forgave him. At Lot 10, Aunt Cil folded the tweed coats and caps and put them away.

The boys returned to their school, perhaps the aunts gave some excuse, perhaps people assumed that they would go away in August at the end of the regular school year. Rudolf at eight years old had been his father's shadow for the short time that Jimmy was around on that visit, and then suddenly nothing. He had sketched the sailing ship that he would travel on; he even knew its name, the Maraval. Children do not forget.

In school holidays, the grandfather made the boys help him repair his houses, so they could learn a useful trade, he said. Sir Carrie built houses and he lent money to people who put their houses up as security. When they could not repay their loans, he became the owner of those houses, repaired them and rented them. With his life a constant cycle of usury, he became hard-hearted, rich and intolerant of laziness. Most people, including his daughters feared and hated him.

As they grew, Rudolf showed a talent for music and hid from his grandfather's chores to read or study or play whatever instrument he got his hands on. Soon they grew into men who no longer needed a mother or father and Carl ran away to the bush rather than be his grandfather's slave. The fatherless Sonny showed a talent for wood and became Sir Carrie's faithful apprentice.

The way they tell the story, grandfather had everyone's slot preordained. When Rudolf brought home good school reports or notes of praise from his teachers, the old man would smile cryptically and say:

"Boy, you're so smart, I'm sure you could teach them teachers a thing or two." Poor Rudolf would struggle to disclaim, but the old man would grumble:

"Come, learn something really useful," and shepherd him toward the rental account books. "Good at book learning, you'll be my accountant!"

There was the day an impatient Sir Carrie came to the school, and though Rudolf tried to slide low in his seat and disappear, the old man strode onto the stage and called him out.

Rudolf never went back, but he lost himself more in music. He never joined the militia nor wore a smart uniform like his father, whose formal band portrait still graced the family album.

Rudolf had a reputation as a good dance band drummer and a virtuoso at all the latest dance steps.

At first, the old man did not mind the music business or the late nights, as long as Rudolf was with him early next day on the job. He was grooming his successors; he wanted them to be shrewd and smart about land, and property and money.

The three fatherless boys fought each other, took the old man's abuse and bided their time. Sonny at last felt himself ahead of the orphaned boys whose parents had deserted them.

Carl found diamonds in Mazaruni. He came to town sporting a gold watch, bought himself a car and learned to drive it, and came with a lot of fuss to take the aunts for a drive one Sunday. Grandfather politely declined. When the money ran out, Carl went back into the bush to try his luck again.

Rudolf fell out with the grandfather, said he wanted his own life and disappeared until the old man died in 1938. Only then, did he come back to the aunts, and put in many months helping them repair the property. They let him open a bicycle repair shop for himself under the bottom house of the cottage in front.

I knew my Uncle Rudolf with his bicycle shop that was a gathering place for gaffers and a domino club. Rudolf bought himself a stylish Raleigh Ensign bike and was always seen shining its chrome with a chamois, and putting gadgets on it, bits of fur about its crossbars, a ticker so that he had a distinctive sound when he rode it. You could hear him whistling various tunes as he worked repairing other people's bicycles. He would work out arrangements for his combo that played gigs at night.

He had promised to teach me how to ride a bicycle so I would wait around the shop, and my mother would call me in to do my homework. It was not proper for a small girl to wait around a place where men gaffed and drank rum and played dominoes loudly into the night.

There must have been women in Rudolf's life, he was now nearly forty, but he never introduced any one in particular to the aunts. When he felt good, you knew it; he drank his rum, he whistled, he played his drums.

The barber would come on his bike to give haircuts to the men and boys of Lot 10. Mr. Eric, plump, clean shaven and serious would hang his razor strop on a nail, take out his white covering cloth, and setting his brown leather bag on a box beside him, would begin to work on the man or small boy sitting in the chair in front of him.

He set up outdoors to cut Rudolf's hair and then he would stay for a round or two of dominos with the fellows in the bicycle shop. Holiday season haircuts were risky because Rudolf was often drunk. The children in the yard would gather to watch. Suddenly, Uncle Rudolf would spring from the barber's chair, and yell, "Merry Christmas!" to the delight of the laughing children. The razor was dangerously sharp and Mr. Eric would try, but Rudolf did not seem to register the danger of losing an ear. Mr. Eric put away his stuff and decided to join Rudolf in a drink. That was the time he bare his soul.

"I am a dangerous man. I grew up all by myself, without a father or a mother. Self made. If you go to the Tower Hotel, they know me there. All the dancers know that I am the best drummer in the world."

Mr. Eric nodded and swirled his rum in his glass. He knew about the drums, but this business of the mother and father made him worry that Rudolf would go from happy to sad drunk too soon. This was a family yard, he knew, and he supposed it had its skeletons, but Rudolf was going rather deep to way back when.

Then Rudolf started to dance for the children. Snapping his fingers and twisting his knees, he tried to get one of the little girls watching to dance with him. She pulled away and ran off giggling.

"Does she know who she is refusing?" he turned to the crowd, speaking loudly but very clearly, despite his drunken state.

"Don't bother with her; she's a little stupid girl," Mr. Eric interceded, pouring another tote from the bottle of rum.

"I am the reigning Jitterbug King" he exclaimed regally and all of the children laughed and clapped, as he strutted about to music only he could hear.

In truth, he used to win dance contests at the various hotels, for jive and bebop, and jitterbug, and the prizes were usually bottles of whisky or rum that disappeared among his domino cronies. Ever since his partner had married and left, everyone thought he had put his dancing days behind him.

It was now 1958, the year his father Jimmy died leaving the insurance policy that Irene used to make her trip back home after thirty-six years. It turned out that when Aunt Cil got the news and told him, Rudolf wrote his mother to ask her help in boosting his bicycle repair business. Irene did not write her son, but in a letter to her sister said that these boys should be coming to her assistance since she was old and had suffered so.

Aunt Cil should have kept her mouth shut, the only prudent thing to do, but she told Rudolf his mother had refused.

The big drunk that everyone remembered lasted all day and all night. Rudolf gave speeches from the front of the yard to the back of the yard; his aunts could not tempt him with food or get him to lie down in his bed, he would spring forth with new ideas and expressed them loudly for the whole yard to hear.

He was going to educate all of his nieces and nephews; their parents had only to ask and he would provide the funds. He had money saved for universities to make their children doctors, lawyers, biochemists.

When the children laughed, their parents told them to hush, and everyone said, "Poor Rudolf!"

Someone suggested getting him to hospital, but he was not ailing, and if someone suspected he was mad he might end up in the asylum in Berbice. His aunts did not want such a thing to happen. They wanted him to calm down, to eat something, to sleep.

The children in the yard had laughed because no one remembered Rudolf being generous or having money. He was never the one to ask a child to run an errand, and say, "keep the change."

The happier memories were of his brother, the one that had struck diamonds and had brought everyone presents and taken them out for rides in his car.

All Rudolf owned was a small canvas cot, his beloved Royal ensign bicycle, his drums and a couple of cardboard suitcases that he stored under the cot. These suitcases disappeared from time to time whenever his aunts missed him, a few weeks or months, when they assumed some woman gave him comfort.

No one had a telephone in the yard so that in a time of crisis you could not call an ambulance. Word spread and a boy ran to the corner for Mr. Norman's hire car to rush him to the hospital. Two women in the yard had first run to his aid. Was he hurt, was he drunk? Seeing the brown beer bottle, smelt it and realized that Rudolf had drunk formalin.

They found him twisting and contorted, groaning a low groan; the sound that brought them upstairs was that of a wounded animal, a dog with its foot trapped, the neighbor said. She held Rudolf's head on her lap, and the other poured soapy water down his throat.

Milk, someone else said. Milk and eggs is what you give for poisoning. Most of the soapy water was a mess of bubbles on the floor beside his head and soaking through Dora's frock. He held his teeth clenched, and his face was drenched with tears and sweat. They managed to get him into the back seat of Norman's car. The driver was a new fellow whose only concern was saving Norman's upholstery, and the women had to threaten him to get him to help maneuver Rudolf into the seat, his head still on Dora's lap.

She was thinking how she would scold him, when this was all over, how she would chastise him for giving them all such a scare. She did not want to look at his agonized face, she only wanted the driver to hurry, past the leisurely bicyclists and the slow dray carts, and get him to the hospital. Two porters in khakis came up as the car approached. One opened the car door and immediately took charge.

"Hurry, hurry," Dora sighed, shifting Rudolf's head onto the seat, and folding her soiled dress inwards.

"Nothing to do," said the porter, "he dead!!!"

Dora wondered how she could have missed it, the moment of death as he lay on her lap. She recalled no stiffening, nor even when his moaning sounds had ceased. She could not hold back the silent tears.

When the aunts decided to open Rudolf's cardboard suitcase, his precious grip that he never allowed anyone to touch; they saw three dress shirts, one with the ostentatious frill front of his dancing contests, and two plain white ones. Sheet music and a Bible were the only other contents.

From inside the cover of the bible a single sheet of notepaper protruded; ordinary paper torn from an exercise book that children use in school. An apology to his aunts; he thanked them for all they tried to do, said he was sorry, and signed himself, not Rudolf, but :

Jimmy, dance band drummer and jitterbug king .

He seemed to have gotten all the ages of his life mixed up, and his Aunt Cil did all of her crying at that point.

They laid him out in Merriman's funeral parlor in his black pants and white dress shirt. He looked darker than usual against the clean starched whiteness of the shirt. His face was a dull mask and they had stuffed cotton up his nostrils, his lips were an even darker black.

Not even a serge suit to be buried in, grumbled a neighbor, a whole life wasted.

The Anglican archbishop forbade the family priest from officiating at his burial. Rudolf had not died in a state of grace, they said, and could not lie in sanctified ground.

Rudolf was dead and past all caring, but the aunts suffered this shame. They had raised him in the church, he had even been a choirboy at one time, and this was their reward. The priest had come in private to their home to offer comfort, but in this final ceremony, they were alone.

They did not know what was suddenly so wrong with the life that Rudolf led; this Jimmy business was all so long ago. They always welcomed him, let him come and go as he chose, gave him a roof over his head, and food to eat, and never pried.

RED JANET

Michael Forde's finger flew the half block distance from Robb Street to Brickdam and landed with its signet ring still attached in the backyard of Miss Ulene Bobb. There was debris and dust and shattered glass, a screeching sound then a boom. It blew out glass windows of grand houses as far as South Road, but it failed to destroy Party Headquarters sufficiently to put them out of operation.

There was the wail of sirens as the ambulance fire engines came, noise and screams from people surging forward against police restraints. Soldiers cordoned off the scene holding people back and collecting evidence. Surely it was a bomb, but who had set it?

Next day the Party newspaper out as usual, headlining its triumphs and plans, passed it over. A small article, almost hidden, mentioned an act of civil disobedience where perpetrators had blown themselves up in an aborted bomb blast.

The youth arm of the movement mourned Michael; the candlelight vigil from Brickdam to the Bourda Green had to end by the eight o'clock curfew. The speakers who declared him a martyr, berated their enemies, and condemned his untimely death, had to cut their sermons short and scramble away when the vans of soldiers arrived to disperse them.

Back in the slum yards of Alberttown neighbors crowded into the little cottage where Michael's mother was still raising his young siblings without a father, and lamented with her:

Michael gone, Michael gone...

Just when the boy of an age to give you something back, look what happen.

What will politics do for you now?

Will politics put bread on the table, food in the mouth of your starving children? So he is a martyr, but where is Red Janet now?

Michael's mother was without tears; Michael was lost a long time ago, and she had reconciled.

The Fordes once owned all the land from Albert Street on the left hand side, right up to Light street corner.

Their grandmother, Mother Braithwaite used to make sweet drinks and mauby to sell in her cake shop. She had the perfect location; right in the middle of the block with two primary schools, at the south end Queenstown, RC and the north side, St Ambrose.

When school let out at lunchtime, you could not stick a pin in the cake shop -- orders for mauby, custard blocks, sugar cake, sweet bread, and buns were coming in fast and furious.

So how come, now that Michael is dead, the family is so poor and hand-to-mouth?

A lot of story happen in between, a lot of story...

There is Mother Braithwaite's son, Michael's father, a drunk and a wastrel, gone... and good riddance!

Poor Michael, trying to be a son and a father at the same time. He had only one year of secondary school before he joined lithographic and trained as a printer; a skill that he brought to the youth movement of the party and a paycheck he gave to his mother.

Politics awakened Michael's dreams for his future. He went on the retreats, printed and distributed tracts, took the Trade Union classes, studied history and political philosophy, read and reread the pamphlets and books.

At first his mother and grandmother welcomed his interest in reading and study. He told them he would get a scholarship to go abroad to study law or engineering. They were happy that he was not carousing and drinking like so many young men.

When his mother realized that the books in his bookcase were Communist material, she knew that he was in the clutches of Red Janet, lured by the promise of study in East Germany or Russia. She knew she had lost her son.

ESCAPE

In January of my sixth form year at Bishops, I was awarded a scholarship to an American college. The telephone message asked me to report to the American consulate, at my earliest convenience.

I have scant recollection of the details, except that the person I saw looked at my file and congratulated me with such enthusiasm because I had won a scholarship worth thousands of American dollars: tuition, room and board, a book and clothing allowance, and airline tickets. They wanted me to travel immediately to be enrolled for the second semester at Connecticut College. It was all quite overwhelming, but in my own mind Bishops culminated in the A' levels which I had been preparing to take in six months.

I did not even know where Connecticut was, but I was worried that my hesitation would make me lose this opportunity to escape. My mother's comment was matter of fact:

"If they want you in January they will want you in September."

So I dutifully took down all the information and wrote a letter to the Institute of International Education which was administering my scholarship and asked to defer until

September because of my G.C.E. exams. I also wrote to Connecticut College thanking them for selecting me and asked for as much information as possible about the college and the town so that I would be properly prepared to join them.

The local newspapers ran articles about me and the two other winners of U.S. scholarships, both men, who were not waiting, but leaving at once for places in Ohio and Minnesota.

It turned out that some new American initiative had taken place as a counterbalance to the scholarships to East Germany and Russia that were being offered to members of the youth arm of Dr. Jagan's socialist party.

battle for the young minds

I had never belonged to any political party and my parents were not active either. When I asked at the U.S. consulate I was told that my examination scores when I applied for some training scholarships advertised the year before were passed on to the international agency and had attracted favorable attention.

I broke my good news to my teachers at Bishops only to have my joy soured by their expressed prejudice against American education in general.

"Their standards are not as good as the British universities" one teacher said.

" I hope you will not slack off in your work because you have a very good chance at a British university place."

I knew that I did not want to go to the U.W.I, I always wanted to get far away from the pettiness of local or Caribbean squabbling about class and kin, and I had set places like Edinburgh and Bristol as goals because my teachers had been educated there.

Now the idea of America and a liberal education, choice of a variety of subjects, began to seem like a welcome relief from the competitiveness of the specialist grind...pure math, applied math, physics that I would be committed to continuing in the drab, wintry moors of Britain.

Whenever I seemed joyful and relaxed, my teachers applied snobbery about British education and accused me of complacency because I had that offer in the US.

I recall charming hand written notes from Dean Elizabeth Babbott welcoming me to Connecticut College; and Robert Cobbledick, the admissions director, sent postcards that showed the campus, and Ocean Beach a famous local attraction.

I liked the Dickensian ring of their names and the cozy friendliness of the little notes. I began to look forward to going there for purely nonacademic reasons: I had no idea what the students or faculty were like or what the academic strengths of the place were; it was near enough to New York and Boston where we had relatives and the people seemed kind.

I arrived in America three days before the momentous March on Washington. My first stop was at Yale University for two weeks in a Fulbright orientation program. On the magnificent campus of Yale, (a school everyone had heard about, and impressed even the snobs at Bishops) I was one of six undergraduates among elite representatives from countries as disparate as Norway and Japan.

I had been relieved by everyone's friendliness because I had been reading all about the Civil Rights demonstrations and had no real sense of the geographic range of emotions on the issue.

I knew about Little Rock and the National Guards called out to integrate schools and universities. I knew of boycotts and sit-ins and disorder but I hoped it was all in a different place and would not affect me. After a fine lunch a group of us sat in a common room and watched the television news of the march; I heard Dr. Martin Luther King and I knew that history was being made.

The campus green was a pastoral fantasy. Reality was out there in the streets. Involvement was not a matter of choice. I was committed by the color of my skin. I thought I had escaped but I had simply joined a greater battle and needed to arm myself to meet it.

WILL'S STORY

We were just sitting there in Brooklyn enjoying a rum, the cold weather locked outside, talking about home.

"I could be under a coconut tree, the sea breeze blowing through my hair."

"Just as long as you're not too near the sea," Will countered, "it is so polluted on those beaches now that you have to worry about the smell."

"Oh, no. There will always be beautiful island beaches." Selwyn drawled stretching his arms out along the back of the sofa. "The tourists aren't going to hog them all!"

"I won't be so sure," Will said, laughing but wagging in warning, "the entire island is a giant golf course for tourists. Everything local got to give way. Even the flying fish are flying south!"

And we all took another rum and swapped stories. Will had the floor.

"I step off the plane at JFK and see this little dog in a green jacket, so cute his floppy ears almost touching the ground, a beagle type of dog. And he come up around my feet, looking up with his little red eye, and here is me, clucking my lips friendly, and reaching down:

"Come doggie, here doggie !"

Me, not realizing that the dog was on the job, hanging around my ankles, sniffing me for his masters.

"This way , sir." A customs officer appear out of nowhere. A pinched face white guy, Polish, the name on his uniform nameplate say " something-ski". I am confused, why is he leading me off to the side? I can't even get my voice to say anything, and I see my suitcase getting a different mark from the other ones nearby.

"Are you carrying any meat, fruit, vegetables? Agricultural products of any kind? And he is looking straight into my face.

I just finish filling out "No." to the same kinds of questions on the customs sheet, and I can't be sure whether I still have the form in my passport or if somebody collect it already. I am thinking fast, and then I decide to say "No."

The officer reach and took my passport, and started studying it. He is reading everything, I swear, every page in the passport, every stamp. All this time I getting annoyed and starting to sweat. All these years I travelling, this kind of thing don't happen to me."

"So, what happen," Selwyn breaks in, getting impatient and pouring himself a long rum. Will is famous for dragging out these stories and making drama.

"Wait, man," Will continues, setting the scene at his own pace.

"Is this your suitcase, sir" he asked me.

"And this piece your hand luggage?"

What's the use denying anything. I so proud of my matching tweed luggage, my name printed large on both pieces. This is the evidence. And I know that the dog was the one that set me up. I start looking round for the little mutt, I want to kick him now, but he must be off on another case.

I see my suitcase open. This man unwrapping everything my mother packed so carefully, the pickles, the pepper sauce wrapped up in a towel so the bottle wouldn't break. But he is not bothered by these. Then he hits the jackpot. Not even wrapped, just lying at the bottom of the bag, the same way the feller gave them to me. Six sapodillas, brown and hard.

Everybody burst out laughing. Will had got his punch line, they thought. Selwyn almost choked, and poured himself another long rum, he didn't even bother to add a chaser, but Will was not finished, he held up his hand and took the floor again.

.".Wait...and one green mango! Seven pieces of incriminating evidence laid out on the counter. The mango, an insult, so green and hard you could use it for a cricket ball."

Cricket brought back memories of raggedy small boys batting and chasing after the ball barefoot in the hot sun. For a moment, we could really forget that it was winter in a strange country. We mumbled agreement and almost branched out into talking sports, but Will was not finished yet.

The customs officer kept going through the suitcase. I hear somebody laugh but I was feeling too ashamed to look up.

"What's this?" he asked, his voice dead serious. He had come upon my father's clock, one that my mother insisted I bring back as a souvenir. The clock doesn't work but right at that moment I could swear it was ticking.

The man stood back and asked me to remove it. He thought it was a bomb and he finish seeing me as some kind of criminal. I was mad but starting to get frightened too. I decided to make a full confession. The two packages of bay leaf in my shoes, the aloes I was bringing to make painkiller. I just didn't care anymore. The man stopped listening to me and wrote out a slip of paper.

"I am sorry sir, but I did ask you three times, giving you ample opportunity."

Three times like Peter denying Christ, and the fowl cock crowing three times. I am so confused feeling like a lying idiot. What is this the paper says?

A fine of one hundred dollars. One hundred American dollars for useless Trinidad fruit I didn't even want!"

All because of that damn vagrant who stick his head into my taxi when I got to Piarco that morning. I gave him two dollars. After all, I doing well in New York and I feel sorry for the guy. Who told me to be kind? He look at me sad-like and say he really feel like eating a chicken roti which cost six dollars.

"What a gall these beggars have," I said aloud. The taxi driver just laugh and the guy as if to prove that he is not a beggar, empty the fruit on to my lap.

"Take these," he said, "they will be nice when they ripe. But I am hungry now."

So I like a fool gave him my money and bring these crosses to blight me!

I began to complain to the customs officer that I was a poor man, paying my taxes, and right at this minute my son was fighting for Uncle Sam down in the Persian Gulf.

You know, the man listen. He look at me and he reach for the paper.

"Please do not let this occur again, sir."

I thought he was going to give me a break, but anyway, he reduce the fine to twenty-five dollars, so I pay up and collect my stuff quick to get out of there.

"What happen to the fruit? You think I care.. Oh, yes, the officer did ask me what they were called, he was writing out some report.

But just then I spot the dog again. Off-duty, wagging his tail and getting dogging treats from another officer.

"Sapodilla." I said and right then I could feel one of those hard brown things in the palm of my hand bowling straight to the animal head. Boom.

But I suck my teeth, I am too nice a guy.

"How is that spelt?" the officer asked. Forget sapodilla, I come to my senses, after all, what do they know?

"It's kiwi fruit, sir." I said and he was satisfied.

SHANTI'S PARLOUR

The trains don't go through the park anymore. The iron donkeys that the British brought to the colonies still wind their way across India, but they are pretty much gone from the Caribbean where a rented car can cross and re-cross islands in half a day.

In the Guyana of the sixties, train lines spanned the thin coastal strip, reclaimed from the jungle inside and the Atlantic without. This narrow band 50 miles long was where the people lived in tiny villages on sugar estates; the interior, a tangle of rivers and forests, remained vast and unknown to them.

It is now the 80's and I am standing at the park entrance watching the forty-foot canal where every small boy learned to swim, and many drowned, and where Jamie, who got fits, sat one day alone and disappeared. It is as if by standing in the same spot, I can clear my head of clutter.

Pushing aside logic and present times, I can conjure up the sound of the six o' clock train, on its way up the East Coast, slowing down at the park gates, letting off its passengers, the civil servants who worked in the city and lived in the villages.

Depeeza holds his flag and waits in his khaki uniform, his baldhead shines and his stance correct as the soldier he once was. The train stops, it screams, he adjusts his signals, he waves it on.

Not fast and deadening like New York subway trains, not rhythmic like the little engine of the fairy-tale, but sweating and smoking, clanking and whistling and slow it moves on its way. People hang out of the windows, pushing up the wooden shutters to reach out to vendors of bread and fish making their final sales.

Children going home from an afternoon of play, loiter at the park to wave it on. Beyond the park gates, beyond the garden plots of vegetable vendors, the lavish lawns spread out, the private life of the country.

The Portuguese tennis club, the East Indian social club, ringed and barricaded testimony to a less than idyllic social world. When did they abolish the clubs? How long after the incidents?

"The government is determined to look forward."

Those were the actual words and the message of the half hour speech from the Minister of Information who set the scene for the Minister of Economic Development to present his specific plans to the team of potential investors at our conference.

My group, mostly small business and technical support companies based in New York, was of particular interest to the Minister; most of us had grown up in this country or were the children of those who had left and prospered abroad.

They seemed to expect more from us, and to be sure, we seemed to expect special treatment from them. So far, however, I had felt mounting frustration -- I could not penetrate beyond political platitudes and posturing -- the whole venture had been a mistake.

At breakfast that morning in the Woodbine Hotel, where the air-conditioning is turned off in the mornings to preserve their ancient generator, and the big wooden fans wind lazily and uselessly above our heads, my colleague was optimistic.

"Today is the day!" He wagged his finger gleefully.

"I will get my agreement signed, and, after that, it's just processing the details!"

"Those guys are eager for us to start up." he continued, moving his fork deftly among the sausages and eggs on his plate. It was true that there was an unusual display of bounty at the breakfast buffet: juices of every kind, fruit and breads, items that the locals rarely saw or could afford.

"What are you so glum about?" he remarked when he registered my silence.

"I am going to wait; I want to hear what other people have to say." I replied, already resolved to do my own snooping around the few local families that I still kept in touch with in the country.

"Like the minister said, the country is committed to fairness; every racial group will get an equal chance. Look at the cooperation between the Indians and blacks at all levels of the government."

"That's true," I was forced to admit. Not so long ago, there was so much suspicion and backbiting that progress seemed impossible.

"The PM never lets you forget," my companion smiled, his mouth full of food, "the crafty old hypocrite. I have nothing against expediency."

It seemed that everywhere on this visit someone, official as well as ordinary, was making comments about racial harmony, multiracial representation, and fairness at long last. Even the hotel manager had stopped by and contributed his bit.

"This is their game for CARIFTA and the IMF," I commented with skepticism when I heard that cabinet posts were fairly distributed. "And to keep gifts coming from the IDB and other donors."

Everyone spoke with multiple acronyms that everyone else seemed to comprehend.

"Things are going to turn around for Guyana," my friend persisted, "there is real hope and optimism now. All they have to do is build back the infrastructure and development will take off. We are long past the "incidents"; those are times best forgotten."

A surly black waitress was hovering around to clear our table but my companion had taken second helpings and was mowing through a heap of fried plantains on his plate. I had closed my knife and fork on my plate but I toyed with my glass of papaya juice uncertain of exactly what it reminded me of.

It was as if by mutual consent we were observing a moment of silence. After the incidents, there was the great wave of emigration and in a sense; we were all exiles returning after twenty years. In those times, simple villages had become inflamed targets: Indians against blacks, blacks against Indians. This was beyond reason, beyond history.

The slaves had come first to work the sugar fields, then after abolition the Indians came as indentured laborers to do the work the blacks had left behind.

The Portuguese, as merchants and tradesmen had come, exploited both groups and prospered as the owners of most of the businesses.

Now, whatever the government's optimism, the truth was that Indians and blacks remained at the bottom of the colonial class society whose allegiance was to England.

The mystery still unanswered of the sixties was this: how was it that when at last the country became their own, deserved and politically won, Indians and blacks set at each other's throats to destroy it?

I was trying hard to remember what had started the incidents, what exactly had triggered off that violent season we sought now so many years later to suppress. I chided my friend in his use of "incidents."

"Call it tribal warfare, that's what it was."

"Easy girl, easy…" he countered. But it came out in a torrent of frustration.

"That is the government's ploy, put a neutral label on it and you don't have to see it for what it really is. We talk about "the suffrage", "the suspension of the constitution", "the incidents" like chapters in a history book, and not like events that affect people's daily lives, whether they had food to eat, whether their children died."

"Why are you getting so passionate?' he asked. "I am just here for this week, to get my contracts settled then back to my place in the good old U S of A! I am not going to get emotional, this place is not ready for me yet… but it's getting there."

He shook the crumbs from his lap and we rose; the waiter staring after us, two sober and serious returning business-people.

214

I forced myself to laugh at my own emotionalism, but I was
deeply disturbed by memory, and I could not forget that
trains played a major part in the incidents. There was a time
that if a train carried a passenger load of blacks it could not
stop at an Indian village station, when vigilantes of both races
stalked the train yards at dawn and massacres shut down
work for weeks. It was the trains that brought into town the
crude coffins of policemen killed trying to keep order
between black and Indian neighbors.

So it was that instead of the prosaic business for which I had
come, I made my way that afternoon to where the old train
station used to be beside the Lamaha canal in the park.

I see it clearly, as if it were today. I hear the shouts of the
boys coming home at 6 AM not with treasure, but with grief
and tragedy. The entire street, the mothers with anything
thrown over their nightclothes, house slippers on their feet
rushed down to the park to the train master's house.

That was the day that boys had tried to scale the fence of the
East Indian club, looking for odds and ends left after a fair;
wallets, coins, bottles to sell, the usual stuff that small boys
scrounge. Small boys would take an early swim in the forty-
foot canal, and get home as their families were rising.

It was the sort of life for a boy, because the sun rose early
and daily chores would begin for him the moment his parents
were awake.

This day, Depeeza' son, Michael, led the bunch trying to scale the fence. They saw him shake; another boy grasped him only to be thrown back. Then, there he lay, blackened and stiffening, dying on the early morning grass. This was the place, and I see it now, with the grass burned brown where he fell.

What kind of people would electrify a fence? Why something so dangerous in a place where other people come and go? What kind of country do we have, who are we keeping in or keeping out?

These kinds of things the mayor said when he spoke at Michael's funeral. We all heard him, we all stood, in our Sunday clothes at the entrance of the park.

I stood uncomfortable in uncomfortable clothes and watched my playmate not running and jumping as I knew him, but stiff and silent in a monstrous satin casket.

I used to watch Depeeza's wife afterwards, imagining that I saw tears in her eyes as she saw us grow. I was sure that she always wondered what kind of man her son would have grown into if the Indians had not killed him.

I walk into Shanti's parlor and beer garden because my memory led me in this direction and a sudden rain breaks through the sky where the sun blazed just moments before.

Some things resist change and this little shop, its title board painted yellow and blue could easily have occupied this spot thirty years ago before modern music and microwaves.

There is the polished wooden counter, the glass case displaying cakes for sale and a general air of respectable dinginess. As a child, I loved sweet Indian delicacies like meetai and jelabi that used to drip with honey and flies. Now all I wanted was shelter from the short spell of rain.

A record of Hindu popular music is playing softly on the radiogram and the two men in civil servant garb of dark pants and white shirtjac at the far end of the counter seem to be enjoying it. They move their heads in time with the syrupy jingling and shrill whine of a female singer as they silently take the plates offered by a woman in a flowered dress, with a white lace orhni about her head.

She takes their money and walks over to ask what I would like to have.

"Just a soft drink," I say, realizing that I could not just stand there.

"We have Pepsi and coconut water", she replies.

Suddenly I realize how much things have changed. Unlike the days of my childhood when there were many types of soft drinks to choose from, my favorites Lime Rickey's and cream soda in the small bottles that needed an opener to snap off their corks, the country now in the throes of its buy local austerity campaigns, had drastically shrunk the range of items available everywhere.

I chose coconut water, but was not prepared for the thin over-sweet stuff that came out of the bottle she served me with a straw.

Two men in work clothes, mud-colored khaki trousers and shirts, and canvas shoes that marked them as laborers, were seated at a table in a corner of the parlor eating. As I looked over at them, she added:

"We have roti and poori to take-out. Or to eat here, if you prefer."

She didn't quite know where to place me and clearly didn't want to offend. The other patrons were Indian, and I black. I nodded in reply but did not intend to risk my health any further.

Something about the shop was familiar, and I looked around taking in the large colored pictures of Indian deities edged with passé partout that decorated the walls.

When I saw the faded newspaper photographs and the huge colored picture of the dancing girl, I knew that this was the memorial for the little dancing girl from a long time ago.

She was seven, photographed in full costume, bangles around her ankles, hands shoulder high, fingers in tribute to Shiva.

The year that she made all the newspaper headlines, they said that her rendition of the sacred dances were so unique that some thought she was a special reincarnation of Lakshmi.

She was featured that year at every festival, the Pagwah, Mashramani, and the newspapers were hungry for every detail of her life. Her mother told of her eating habits, when she slept and when she woke, how many hours she practiced her dances, that she was so creative that she always added something of her own to whatever dance they taught her.

There was talk of a pilgrimage to India, and the events and activities of the Indian Fair that year were in her honor. She was the main event and a great deal of money was raised for her trip.

Then with no warning the child took ill; engagements had to be canceled. Suddenly the whole country was praying for Shanti. The doctors could find no real cause. It was preposterous that tight clothing could account for the gangrene that set in on her right leg.

To save her life the doctors recommended amputation, but her mother in deep grief with prayer and fasting withheld permission. She was sure of a miracle; Shiva would save the dancer intact for the dance. After more than three weeks of consuming the headlines, Shanti died.

As I drank my drink and waited for the rain to stop, I asked the woman about the child in the picture. "That was my little sister," she said.

As I continued to stare at the picture, she related:

"The shop is named for her. She had a special gift from Shiva, she was only seven but to see her dance ..." and she rolled her eyes to illustrate the ecstasy.

"She is very pretty." I said trying to sound innocent and sincere. "What happened to her?"

"She was killed by evil jealous people. One day she was dancing, next day she was dead. Obeah, they put it on her... black magic," she explained, seeing the incredulous look in my face.

Perhaps she thought that, being a stranger, I would not understand.

QUEEN OF LOT 10

Della marched out of Correia's supermarket with two frozen chickens securely fastened to her middle. Her basket over her left arm contained groceries she had paid for, her staples: a bag of rice, flour, sugar, onions, half pound of salt codfish, a couple of cans of evaporated milk She was stepping gingerly, her arms held away from her body, walking not too fast, but eager to move on. She was a large woman in those days, no soft fat but solid, and as she moved, her high buttocks did their slow roll from side to side. That should keep him busy, she had calculated, and sure enough, the security guard muttered as she nodded and passed him:

"Good day to you, missus," he said, as with a sly smile his eyes moved swiftly from her face and focused on her rolling departure.

With jaw set and head held high, Della stepped onto the pavement and sauntered down the road. These were times to make your head swim with confusion, and it was in one of these states that she had hatched the chicken plan.

For three Saturdays straight, she had been looking at the chickens. She would stand for a long time at the frozen bin, turning them this way and that with her fingers, oblivious to the cold. She would heft one, as if to check its weight, then shake her head as if it did not meet her standards. She knew that she did not have the money to buy.

It took great ingenuity to grab a cold chicken unnoticed and spirit it away, but if you knew anything about Della you were not surprised; she managed to grab two. When it came to a choice between feeding her children and any other consideration, there was no contest.

But it really should not have come down to this level. In regular times, this woman would be at her sewing machine outfitting droves of people for weddings, graduations and special occasions. Yards and yards of tulle, peau de soie, and expensive French lace would foam and billow on her front room floor, and Friday afternoons, precise as clockwork, her clients would line up to pay down the agreed installment for Della's work.

But times changed.

"You tell me, what am I going to sew? Buy local, buy local, and what is there to buy, and with what? We can't wear coconut fibre, and we don't grow cotton and flax!"

Where are the cotton mills and designer clothing factories? These had never got past the politician's dream for development.

The single shirt factory that was struggling to stay afloat had machines forever breaking down from poor maintenance. The promises they made to the young people they had hired were forever unfulfilled, and youth with any talent lined up at the American Consulate to flee the country.

Money was tight for everyone. Della's clientele dropped off, but, even worse, she had completed work sitting in her house that people were not picking up because they could not afford to pay. Old customers seemed to be dodging her, then they just disappeared.

Della was not fussy, as a trained seamstress she could sew anything, men's or women's clothes, school uniforms, shrouds for the dead, she could even weave fishing nets.

But these days people had little money to give for her hard work. Everybody had a relative in America who could send down a barrel of used summer clothes, so a new breed of traders sprang up ready to make a quick dollar selling American castoffs as the latest styles. Sprostons Wharf on Water Street was now the busy place, with everyone redeeming giant clothes barrels and moving them through the town in dray carts.

This is what the new republic had done for them, turned the country into a nation of beggars: everybody waiting for handouts, old clothes, food from overseas, anything they could hustle or trade.

Della's last good work had been an order for a dozen tailored shirt jacks for Mr. Austin, the parliamentary secretary of the Ministry of Trade. His wife had been her staunch client for years and Della was grateful that a door was opening for more government orders to follow.

The Prime Minister himself had led this new revolution in clothing. From now on, the political insiders would abandon European suits and ties and adopt instead Nehru-collared shirt jackets and the less formal open-necked shirt jacks for all their business wear.

Mr. Austin was pleased with his order, but no repeat business came, and Della heard rumors that these same politicians were getting more and more elaborate shirt jackets, with tucks, pleats and embroidery, custom made in England and Hong Kong.

Mrs. Austin and the other government officials wives could afford to dash off to New York or Barbados on shopping jaunts and came back with all the outfits they could ever need. Sometimes they came to Della for alterations, but that was neither steady nor sustaining; the day of the independent seamstress was clearly over. Since she had set up her business she had seen good times and bad, but these were lean years without relief.

Della grit her teeth and almost cried out from the throbbing pain in her upper thighs. Her legs were becoming numb, but she had a few more blocks to walk to get to her house. Today there would be chicken at Della's house again; her scheme had paid off.

What she really longed for was the kind of life that she knew as a girl. No one was hungry and there was always plenty. She was a West Bank girl, acres of fertile river dam where everybody had their own vegetable plot, even plantations that harvested all the produce for market.

Her father was not a rich man, but he was prosperous enough to have a vote on the village council, and on their land, they raised chicken and ducks that they traded for goat meat with their neighbors.

Hunger was unheard of. There was fresh water fish in the creeks and sweet hassar in cane season, and for just a few weeks of work in the cane fields, you had enough money for all other necessities.

This was our life before the modern progress that the politicians promised. Somebody said things had to get worse before they got better. Della sucked her teeth and sighed, better was surely taking its own cool time.

 She remembered how she learned to sew. It was because she wanted something more than village life. To be accepted as a sewing girl, apprenticed to a seamstress, was the height of respectability. It was not like being a servant, it established independence while teaching a good trade.

The madam taught much more than sewing; she showed a girl of sixteen how to know herself, become a full-fledged woman. How to manage a household, handle men, and what proper etiquette was all about…these were what you learned at a good sewing madam, and she exposed you to future clients among the families you met in her home.

Della remembered how excited she felt when she was taken on by Mrs. Boston. Here she was, a plain country girl, decent but not refined, coming to town in her Sunday clothes, with great sweat stains under the arms. She wore rayon, the kind of fabric that did not breathe in the hot midday sun.

How she must have looked, so coarse and country with her unpressed hair and Vaselined knees and elbows; but Mrs. Boston was unfazed and could see her potential:

"My mind take to you, Della, you look like a good, honest girl and I think you could learn this business and do well."

In her three years with Mrs. Boston, she learned fabric inside out, from lace to canvas, and even knew how to make hats to match special outfits. When Miss Boston got special wedding orders, where she had to outfit everybody from the bride and mother of the bride, down to the littlest flower girl, she would train her girls in every aspect of the production.

They would shop for the fabric from wholesalers, examine threads, bias cuts, bolt ends, remaindered swaths of expensive French laces, roll out great lengths and test the selvages with their finger nails, check and recheck, and come away laden with good quality and sure economy.

As her knowledge and tailoring skills grew, Della became a favorite seamstress with clients that requested her special skills in outfitting them. She lost her shyness and in the end, even found a husband.

Byron was not flashy, nor young -- a good steady man with a house in need of a wife. He used to work on a ship and was gone three, four months at a time and his first wife had died in childbirth while he was gone. That made him decide, too late alas, to get a job that kept him home, and now without a wife, he was lonely when Miss Boston introduced Della.

The three children that blessed the marriage made their life complete and Della had the confidence to set up her own dressmaking business in their home. Theirs was a good life before Byron's passing and the hard times that now set upon everybody.

Della wanted to keep up the appearance of good times for her children's sake, and wondered what Mrs. Boston, wherever she was, would think of her actions today in Correia's store. Poor Byron must be turning in his grave to see how far his wife had stooped.

The children were at school when Della came home. Only the stray dog, Flossie, that her youngest son had recently adopted was hanging about the back door, and if she was not mistaken, Flossie looked rather fat, which could mean only one thing.

"As if I didn't have enough trouble feeding these ravenous boys of mine, now a dog with pups!"

But she did not have the heart to shoo Flossie away when she looked up with such pitiful eyes and swung herself under the back steps.

Della put her market basket on the kitchen counter and limped into her bedroom. She loosened the strings around her waist and the sack that fitted like a petticoat about her middle fell to the floor. Weighted by its frozen burden it made a thud on the bare floor.

She picked up the flour bag sack and retrieved the chickens, sucking her teeth as she realized how small they were. Broilers, no good for roasting, not like the sturdy chickens she used to raise. She put them in the sink and turned on the tap.

She would boil them, make soup with the feet, bones and neck, cook the rice in the rich broth, then make curry and Chow Mein with the flesh. She could see four days of family meals, and what a great feast after weeks of beans and rice with just an occasional egg or bits of shrimps.

Even Flossie would have cause for celebration today, and Della felt no remorse. She had come through this venture, she was safely home, so why should she doubt.

God provides in mysterious ways, she reminded herself, and other ways were bound to open to see them through these hard times.

THE LAST KITE

After August, came Christmas then we had Easter.

From the start of each new year, we looked to the next festive season and began to dream of kites. We had a three-month wait, through the dross of the rainy season days of flood, and the colds we were sure to contract afterwards.

We livened the tedium of schooldays with talk and competing plans for our kites.

My brother, Victor, filled his exercise books with sketches of the singing engine he was going to fly; but he and my father could not agree on the dimensions. Vic wanted a gigantic kite, almost as tall as himself but my father, T-square in hand and pencil behind his ear tried to illustrate to his little accomplice what the trade off would have to be:

"Even if we got really light wood, this thing would be too clumsy and wouldn't fly!"

"So you have to choose! A big kite will have to be a frill kite."

Vic looked disappointed, but he was illustrating on the drawing model and marking heavy lines with his pencil:.

"When we add on the buttress here, for a singing engine, we going to get a top-heavy bird."

Most afternoons went by in the planning and making of kites. My mother had admired a box kite last year and my father had been researching the specifications and gathering materials to make her one. Our family usually went to the sea wall with no more than three kites because the girls were not serious about the sport.

We all helped in making kites. My father and brother were the chief designers. They did the actual building of the kite frame with my father's carpentry tools, but everyone worked with paper, cloth and string, cutting out bulls and frills and tying rags on rope to make kite tails.

We girls were happy to have a kite strapped to our back and have our friends admire us, but once on the sea-wall, once the kite was launched in the air, the idea of standing in one place trying to make it stay aloft or free it from entangling other kites, did not seem like fun. We preferred to walk about socializing with our friends.

The tradition of rising early for Easter Monday kite flying came from the Resurrection. On Easter Sunday, church services were as early as 5 AM and new clothes and Alleluias at daybreak seemed fitting. Easter Monday was a day for parades, picnics, parties, and kite flying.

We hardly slept; it was a mark of honor if your kite-laden troop hit the road while it was still dark. We took up our place on the sea wall to launch our kite high in the air just as the sun was rising! My mother had to wake even earlier to cook and pack the picnic food. We took kites and basket and walked along the darkened Lamaha Canal, giggling and shuffling on the pavements as we hit the seawall from its Camp street entrance.

With the wide spread of ocean and the miles of concrete wall framing the beach, this ideal site, awesome in its beauty if you saw it early, was soon overwhelmed. Music in the bandstand and strolling revels, hordes of families picnicking and kites of all shapes and sizes took over the skies. The sea wall was the kite flying Mecca because it had few electrical wires or trees; and Easter Monday was the day.

I well remember my father's glee when all of our kites were launched without problems and he stood back and watched them rise, or swoop, their tails swinging jauntily as they mounted above other kites. The box kite had been a challenge; it tottered like a drunken crate and almost broke as it hit the ground again.

My father had wanted to surprise my mother and had made many practice runs in our nearby park, but today it disappointed him and he fiddled with its loops in frustration. Then he put it aside for a moment and helped launch the others. I took my turn at launching, usually a frill kite, which was a flat hexagon with crepe paper frills on its upper edges. I would place my fingers at the center of the frame in back and walk away from my father in the direction he indicated. He had made the mounting loops at the central pin, and he held the ball of twine in his hand and adjusted the tension before he gave me the signal to let go.

"Be careful with the tail", he would shout, and I would make sure that the tail was unencumbered, then holding my kite above my head, I would let go and watch it rise. With a buzz of its frills it takes off and I am watching as my kite joins the other crazy colored birds in Easter sky.

I race back to take the ball of twine from my father and feel the tautness of the string and know that I am part of this celebration, flying my kite and watching its tail swish and sway with the wind. If another kite string overlaps, I can move my ground position and be in the clear again, but if it strays way out and catches a tree branch or tails entangle or a more aggressive kite brings it down, I have to look for my father or brother's help in its rescue.

Vic is usually with the competitive boys flying complicated kites: whose singing engines hum the loudest, who launched his kite the fastest, whose kite has risen the highest. These boys have learned many complicated loops, have waxed their twine for strength, fortified their kite tails so that their kite is the aggressor and would never be cut away in a tangle. My father would launch again my rescued kite and let my sister take a turn at flying it.

I was never made for serious kite flying and preferred once the initial launch and sky display, to rove about; see what people wore; who was dancing with whom; and what they were saying. Then we had the food: chicken legs, and roti and curry, delicious and easy to eat with fingers.

In the year that my baby brother was three, my father wrapped the ball of twine around his waist and sat him in the middle of the playground. The kite was swinging in the heavens above him and he was giggling in delight. Nearby, my mother organized the picnic food and looked up every now and then to see how my father was progressing with her box kite, which she was eager to fly. He had managed to launch it after changing the loops and slicing off bits of its frame with his penknife, and though it never rose very high, it floated in its own unusual rhythm and stood out conspicuously among the more ordinary kites.

When people stopped by to admire it, how it darted and leapt, how little there was to it, how light it was, my father took credit for its design and my mother for its decoration with blue and red cellophane. Elsewhere along the sea wall we admired the dragon kites, the airplane kites and the woman sized lady kite that no-one had ever seen fly. This year its owner had added a companion for her, a man-sized kite, well painted with all its details. We never saw the launching of the lady and man kites, who knows if they were meant to fly, but like everyone else, we gathered around to gawk.

That was the last Easter Monday our whole family spent happy together. My father had started two jobs to make ends meet and had no time to make kites. Another year, my mother was ill and had an operation around Easter time; my brother was the only one who took up our uncle's invitation to go kite flying.

The last Easter of my father's life, he sat among old men in the Homestead. After the girl that they paid extra to feed him had come and spooned his oatmeal porridge into his eager mouth, she put him in the wheel chair that Cookie had bought.

Someone had left a radio on but he was not listening to the news. His own life confused and full of images flooded his mind. His hands began their restless picking at his clothes, lingering at his crotch. They had him dressed in shorts, it was easier to wash when he soiled them, and his stick legs protruded, the skin dry and shiny and purplish gray.

Andy, who grew up next door and became a deacon, came to give him communion. Andy has learned humility; once a golden boy, it is clear that he has found a direction in his life and I envy him. Nothing fazes him; he is at ease and radiates a caring sense when he deals with people.

My father, who has never bothered much with the spiritual, is now visibly moved. He is fearful now at the end, and as Andy places his hand on his head, you could see almost see tears come; he has spent many months in forgetting but he knows that the end is near, he remembers everything and he is powerless to change anything that has happened in his life.

Victor had this great idea that he would come, lift my father into the car, and have them drive along the seawall. Then he would take him out and have him sit on the wall and watch the kites soar, and listen to the merriment and remember when we were children and we spent our Easter Monday in the same way.

Victor's plan is foolish. It is too late for my father to enjoy anything; his last kite flew when we were still children.

Is it?

TIT BITS

MIRTHFUL DRAMAS, ANECDOTES,

TIT BITS

Entertainment with Abundant Amusement for Guyanese Creoles, at Home and Overseas,

being well interspersed with Creolese of right vintage by

C.A. FARRIER

Price: Combination of Issues No. 1 & No. 2 $1.00

No: 1..50 c. No.2..60 c.

Contents Include

Drama:	Rivalry In Romance or The Trials of Lover Obadiah Jupiter
,,	Grandchild on Order from Ma Ethel
Anecdote:	Mock Court No Entertainment for Dan
,,	Eternal be our Love, O Brother
,,	Sloans Liniment a Sure Cure for Ringworm
,,	Exhausted Hospitality
,,	Pick-Pocket Grabs Novel Booty
,,	The Cruising Commode
,,	The Back-Slider Parrot and Her Reformer
,,	Monkey Dispenses Justice
,,	'Oman' An' Money
,,	Barbadian Brother Johnson no Leader in Prayer
,,	War! Foo Foo Mortar Stick vs Flaming Fire Wood Weapon.

Guyana means Land of Many Waters

The Young Marrieds Club

A House on Laluni Street

A Boy's Life

Fresh Fruits & Vegetables

Rural Church & Cemetery

Porkknockers

The Seawall

School Children

ABOUT THE AUTHOR

Philippa Perry was born and raised in the pre-independence days of British Guiana -- the only English speaking country in South America. She recounts her early days as the second daughter in a family of six children in a struggling middle class family.

Her stories come from a lost civilization of pre-independence stability just as the anarchic blessing of democracy came to the Caribbean.

She recounts her Sisyphean trials growing up a Carrington in Lot 10, First Street, Georgetown -- from the women's battles to the neighbours that never wore clothes to the relatives who walked with their shoes in their hands.

Philippa received her PhD in Psychometrics and became a Bunting Fellow at Radcliffe Institute, Harvard University.

She lectured in Mathematics at University of Guyana and subsequently, at Queens College (NY) for too many years.

Philippa has returned often to Guyana, but, these days, primarily for funerals. She currently resides in Pound Ridge, NY where she spends her time chasing deer from her garden.

Made in the USA
Lexington, KY
31 March 2012